YOUR FUTURE AS A WORKING WOMAN

YOUR FUTURE AS A WORKING WOMAN

By
GLORIA B. STEVENSON

RICHARDS ROSEN PRESS, INC.
New York, New York 10010

Published in 1975 by Richards Rosen Press, Inc.
29 East 21st Street, New York, N.Y. 10010

Copyright 1975 by Gloria Stevenson

FIRST EDITION

Library of Congress Cataloging in Publication Data

Stevenson, Gloria.
    Your future as a working woman.

    Includes bibliographies.
    1. Women—Employment—United States. 2. Vocational
guidance—United States. I. Title.
HD6058.S665   331.7'02   74–22167
ISBN 0–8239–0307–9

Manufactured in the United States of America

To Susan, with thanks for encouragement
and support above and beyond the call.

Acknowledgments

Thanks to Neal Rosenthal and Isabelle Streidl for reviewing the manuscript for this book and to Don Smyth, Ellis Rottman, and Gary Campbell for lending assistance with photographs. Special thanks to Mary DeLaVergne for doing an outstanding job of typing the manuscript and for giving both the project and the author much needed interest, enthusiasm, and support. Thanks, too, to Carmen Johnson for help with proofreading.

About the Author

GLORIA STEVENSON is a writer for the *Occupational Outlook Quarterly,* a career information magazine published by the Bureau of Labor Statistics of the U.S. Department of Labor. In this post, she has reported on a wide variety of topics related to the world of work, but her interests—stemming largely from her own experience as a girl and woman—have prompted her to specialize in articles about job opportunities and the problems faced by women in their careers. Topics she has covered for the *Quarterly* include the need for high-school girls to plan careers, new opportunities for women in police work and the armed forces, and the high unemployment rate among black teenage girls.

Ms. Stevenson joined the Department of Labor in 1967 after earning a bachelor of arts degree in English from the Pennsylvania State University. Elected to Phi Beta Kappa, she has first-hand knowledge of the social pressures that prompt women to fear academic success, as well as of the conditioning that says woman's place is in the home. As she writes in her preface, she grew up thinking she did not need to *plan* her future, because some day a man would come along and *be* her future.

Ms. Stevenson is a member of the American Personnel and Guidance Association and the National Organization of Women. She also serves as an adviser to a paraprofessional program offering training to editing and publications assistants through George Washington University's Continuing Education for Women program.

Preface

This book is written for two groups of girls: those who expect
to hold paying jobs for a good many years of their lives, and those
who do not. No matter which view they hold while young, both
groups of women are likely to be in the work force for a substantial
number of their adult years.

This book cites many statistics about women's work patterns
that support this prediction. It also includes facts and figures
about the labor market, occupations and occupational trends,
earnings, and other aspects of employment. Much of this information was compiled by the Bureau of Labor Statistics of the U.S.
Department of Labor. Many other facts about women's work
patterns came from the Labor Department's Women's Bureau and
from the U.S. Bureau of the Census. However, the ideas expressed
around and about the federal data used in this book are my own.

I want to state, too, that this book is frankly biased. It reflects
opinions, value judgments, and theories that spring partly from
my work in the field of occupational and career information, and
partly from my own experience as a girl who grew up thinking
she did not need to plan her future, because one day a man would
come along and be her future. Feminist and counseling literature
suggests that this attitude is still all too prevalent among young
women.

Foremost among the prejudices in this book is the strong belief that work can be, but often is not, a fruitful, satisfying activity offering workers personal identity, feelings of self-worth, avenues for self-expression, opportunities for growth, and good pay. I hold that women have the right to these rewards; and I believe that women who realistically appraise themselves and the labor market, and who have the courage and know-how to seek the job satisfaction they want, stand a good chance of reaching their goals.

I maintain, too, that many of society's notions about women and work effectively prevent millions of women from exploring a wide variety of employment options that could be both personally and economically satisfying. Among such notions are the beliefs that woman's place is in the home or in home-related jobs and that women have aptitudes for certain skills but lack the capacity to learn others. Some jobs are said to be inherently "feminine" and others are "masculine." Another notion is that women cannot find as much satisfaction in work as they can in family relationships. It is also considered "unfeminine," by some, for women to seek or achieve success in their work. I sincerely hope this book will encourage readers who still agree with these beliefs to question their validity, and, where personally appropriate, to look to new employment horizons.

GLORIA STEVENSON

Contents

Acknowledgments   vii

About the Author   ix

Preface   xi

I.   Women and Work   3
     How Long Are You Likely to Work? — The Rewards of
     Work — Long-term Career Planning

II. Learn About Yourself   17
     Taking a Personal Inventory — Determining Your Aptitudes
     — Examining Your Character Traits — Recognizing Your
     Values — Considering Physical Limitations and Assets —
     Obtaining an Outside Opinion — Effects of Personal Change

III. Investigating Occupations   38
     Aspects of Various Employment Fields — Characteristics of
     Occupational Information — Sources of Information

IV. Where Women Work   58
     Occupational Fields and Workers — Why Women Work in
     Certain Fields — Better Employment Fields for the Future

V.   Preparing for Work   75
     Types of Job Skills — Acquiring Skills — Where to Acquire
     Skills — The Necessity for Some Type of Training — How
     to Choose Job Training — Once You Have Chosen

VI. Finding a Job   109
     Preparation for the Hunt — Preparing a Résumé — Find-
     ing Employers — Applying for Work — The Interview

VII.   *What to Expect in the Workplace*   136
*Responsibilities — Personal Attitudes — Obligations of the
Employer — Laws Concerning the Employment of Women*

VIII.   *Moving Up*   150
Advantages and Disadvantages — Looking for Advancement

IX.   *Combining Work and Family*   162
*If You Marry — Who Does the Chores? — If You Become a
Mother — Going Back to Work — Should You Be a Work-
ing Mother?*

YOUR FUTURE AS A WORKING WOMAN

CHAPTER I

Women and Work

Most teenage girls have at least a vague idea of the role that work will play in their lives. Which of the following expectations comes closest to your own?

1. You are seriously interested in a long-term career, and you plan to work throughout your life, whether or not you marry or have children.

2. You plan to get a job after high school or college, and you may or may not know what kind of job that will be. You want to marry and eventually quit work to have babies. You may want to go back to work, maybe part time, when your children are older, but that possibility seems so vague and far away that you do not seriously think about or plan for it.

3. Your number one aim is to get married. You may work for a short time after leaving school, but you want to quit as soon as possible and devote your life to home, husband, and children.

If you hold the first point of view, congratulations on your determination, and good luck in achieving a rewarding work life. A relatively small but growing number of high-school girls share your strong commitment to work, a commitment that will probably lead you to find many satisfactions in the world of work if you choose a career field that meets your needs. You must prepare for it well and take whatever action is needed—before and throughout your work life—to get what you want from work.

Girls holding the second outlook probably have lots of girl friends who agree with it. This is a common viewpoint among teenage girls, and such expectations will, to some extent, come true. You need to plan and prepare seriously for your early years at work, as well as for that far-off day when you may want to return to work after your children are old enough to take care of themselves, however, if you want your years on the job to be enjoyable, productive, and profitable. Girls and women who drift into and out of the work force without careful planning often find themselves facing poor job prospects, or burdened with jobs they do not enjoy or that pay low salaries.

Girls holding the third viewpoint should wake up! You live in a fairy-tale world—a world in which a beautiful maiden suffers some horrible hardship (work) until rescued by a handsome prince (a husband), who takes her away from the workplace forever. But the real world does not work that way. The prince might never arrive, and, even if he does, work will probably still play an important role in your life. You need to bring your expectations in line with the reality of women's work lives, and plan ahead to cope with that reality.

How Long Are You Likely to Work?

Career planning and preparation are important to all teenage girls, no matter what their expectations about work. The Women's Bureau of the Department of Labor predicts that nine out of ten girls will work outside the home at some point in their lives, and it is estimated that six out of ten will work for up to thirty years. If you doubt that these statistics apply to you, take a close look at what your future is apt to be if women's current work patterns continue.

If your life follows the most common path, you will probably graduate from high school—about eight out of ten girls now do—and you may be among the small but growing number of women who earn college degrees. Fewer than two out of ten women of working age have completed four or more years of college, but the ranks of college-educated women are increasing year by year. Regardless of what kind of education or training you get—or do not get—however, you will probably look for work immediately after you leave school. Nearly 60 percent of all women between 18 and 24 years old are in the work force.

You will probably marry, most likely at a fairly young age. Nine out of ten women marry at some time in their lives, and half do so before the age of 21.

You are also likely to become a mother. Eight out of ten females have at least one child, and half of all mothers have their last offspring before they are 30 years old. If you are in this group, the "baby" of your family will be in school by the time you are in your middle thirties. At that point, either because you enjoy working, because you are bored and lonely staying at home, or because you want—or need—to supplement your husband's income, you are likely to go back to work.

More than half of all women between the ages of 35 and 54 work either part time or full time. The tendency for married women to go back to work during these ages helps to account for the fact that three-fifths of all working women are married and living with their husbands, and that more than a fourth work part time.

Should you return to work at age 35 and bear no more children, you may expect to work, on the average, for about twenty-four years. In other words, you might find yourself combining marriage and a career for nearly a quarter of a century!

That is what lies ahead if your life follows the most common pattern. If it takes other tracks, however, you are apt to find work playing an even bigger role in your life.

For example, you may never marry. About one out of ten women currently remains single. A greater proportion of women may forego matrimony in the years ahead, not for lack of a mate but because changing social values and women's increasing freedom to select a wide range of life-styles may prompt more and

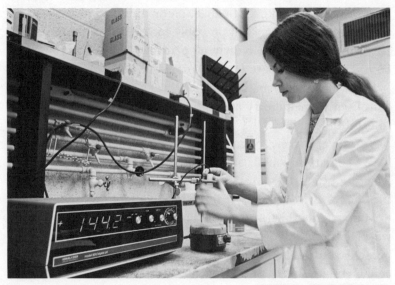

COURTESY U.S. DEPARTMENT OF LABOR

Women who never marry can expect to work for about forty-five years, and those who return to work at age 35 after having children can expect to work for another twenty-four years. The chemical laboratory worker above has chosen a field she hopes to enjoy throughout her work life.

more women to choose a single life. If you do remain single, you can expect to work for about forty-five years of your life.

You may also be the one woman in ten who is widowed before the age of 50, or yours may be among the growing number of marriages that end in divorce. About three out of ten marriages are currently dissolved and divorce rates are rising. In either of these cases, you may well need to work to support yourself or your children.

You might also elect not to have children or be unable to have them. Married women without children are, on the average, twice as likely as other women to be in the work force.

Unless you are already committed to working, you may still find it hard to realize that employment may well play a much larger role in your life than you now imagine, and that you need to make long-term career plans. To bring these facts home, try to imagine yourself in one of the following situations—situations that could occur in any woman's life.

1. You go to work as a computer operator after graduating from high school. After a year you get married, and after another year you leave work to have children. Your husband's job seems promising, but he does not make as much money as you both had hoped. Realizing that one salary just will not cover the rising cost of medical and dental care, savings for the children's education, and the home you want to buy, you try to find a job. Computers have become far more sophisticated than they were when you were working, however, and you find that you are not qualified for available jobs. What do you do?

2. You go to work as a receptionist for a sales company when you are 18. Two years later you marry a handsome salesman, and you quit work as soon as you become pregnant. Your husband travels a lot, is home less and less, and starts playing around with other women. Because his earnings depend on how much he sells, his income is irregular; and he seems to spend more money on the road than he brings home. At age 30, you are so unhappy with the situation that you seek a divorce. The court rules that your former husband must pay a certain amount of money to support your three children, but it is not enough and it also does not arrive regularly. What will you do?

3. You get a college education and teach for several years before marriage, quitting when your first child is due. Your husband has a good job, and things go well until you are 34, when your husband is killed in an automobile accident, leaving you with four children. Your husband had life insurance, but that money does not last long. Meanwhile, the number of trained teachers available in your neighborhood has exceeded the number of jobs, and you find that the schools hire recent graduates in preference to women who have not worked for several years. What can you do?

4. You work as a stewardess after high school and marry a businessman you meet on one of your flights. You quit work, have children, and enjoy the roles of wife, mother, and homemaker for twenty years. You realize one day that your children are grown, you can do each day's housework in a couple of hours, and you have about thirty more years to live. What do you do?

5. You quit college to marry. Your husband has two more years of college to go, and you go to work as a clerk-typist to help put him through school. You are an intelligent person and you find the job dull and unchallenging, but it helps pay the rent and school fees. You quit as soon as you can and have two children. When both are in school, you become bored and lonely staying at home, so you go back to work—again as a clerk-typist. You hate the work nearly as much as you did the first time. You are 38 years old and expect to live until you are 75. What do you do?

6. You become pregnant while in high school and never get your diploma. You live with your widowed mother, who gets Social Security payments, and she takes care of the baby while you go to work in a dry-cleaning shop. The pay is low, but together, you and your mother can support the household. Then your mother gets sick. You cannot afford to pay a baby-sitter to take care of the baby, but you cannot afford to quit work either. How can you cope?

The Rewards of Work

Girls who understand and accept the fact that work may well play a very important role in their lives may not be overjoyed. Indeed, unless your commitment to work is already strong, you may find the prospect of spending many years at work positively grim. This is a natural reaction, for although so many women spend so many years on the job, our society still tends to teach girls to look at the world with a kind of "tunnel of love" vision. In this perspective, husband, home, and children are seen as the most important things in every woman's life, and work and other activities lying outside the tunnel are viewed as offering few, if any, satisfactions.

Moreover, many people, men as well as women, tend to look at paid employment as a necessary evil, not as an activity that can bring a lifetime of satisfaction. In reality, work that matches the interests, abilities, and goals of the individual worker can greatly enrich the lives of women as well as men. You may actually find that you like to work and that the rewards of work are different from those arising from love relationships, but they are nonetheless real.

The most tangible reward of work is, of course, money. Whether married or single, a working woman can pay all or part of the costs of a home, attractive furniture, a car, clothing, dinners out, travel, tennis lessons, stocks and bonds, or any of the other things she might want to buy. A working woman can single-handedly support her children, or she can contribute toward their educations, music lessons, bicycles, braces, or other child-rearing expenses that her husband's income alone may not be able to cover. Moreover, a paycheck has many other benefits, intangible benefits that can add to a woman's sense of self-confidence, strength, and independence.

Our economic system rewards people who do the jobs it wants, needs, and considers important by giving them an income. The nation puts a positive value on this exchange; it is generally considered "good" to be a wage earner. No matter how worthwhile it may actually be, unpaid work such as housework and volunteer activity does not carry the kind of social prestige attached to paid employment. The woman who apologetically introduces herself as "just" a housewife has recognized that society does not award her work the same recognition and dignity it gives paid employment. The working woman, on the other hand, enjoys the social prestige associated with paid work. Secure in the knowledge that society values her work—and says so every payday—she does not need to refer to herself as "just" a stenographer, research technician, or nurse.

A paycheck can also help a woman feel that she is an independent adult who can stand on her own two feet in life and does not need someone else to take constant care of her. Financially, a married woman who does not work is in a purely dependent position, and a person who depends on one other person to meet his or her needs in any area—financial, emotional, or whatever—may eventually feel helpless, unable to take care of him- or herself, and desperately afraid of losing the other's support. Moreover, the dependent person may resent the other for being in a "superior" position, and feelings of resentment are not apt to help build a happy marriage. Married women who work, even part time, avoid total financial dependence and gain satisfaction from knowing that they can help to support themselves and their children.

By contributing to the family's income, the working wife may also gain a greater voice in financial decision-making. In homes where the wife does not work, the husband may have the last word in determining how the family income will be spent because he earns the paycheck. Like financial dependency, this kind of arrangement may make a woman feel like less than an equal marriage partner. The wife who helps to bring home the bacon, however, is apt to have a greater role in determining where each piece will go.

Along with its paycheck-related rewards, work can offer several satisfactions.

1. The chance to develop your own individual talents, skills, and interests. Everyone has aptitudes and tastes that combine to form a unique human being. Work is an excellent arena for developing such individual traits, for the job world needs nearly every talent and skill imaginable and deals with virtually every subject under the sun. By offering you the chance to develop and sharpen your unique traits—an opportunity you may not find in housework—work can provide you with an avenue to lifelong personal growth.

2. An outlet for creativity. Creativity is the development of new ideas, products, or ways of doing things. It is central to such fields as writing, fashion design, architecture, photography, scientific research, and filmmaking, but many other occupations also offer opportunities for creativity. The best business executives, secretaries, lawyers, janitors, and driving instructors, for example, are those able to devise new, more efficient, or more effective methods of doing their jobs or solving problems within their fields. Imagine how you might feel in a job that gives you a chance to come up with new ideas and help turn those ideas into reality. You probably would feel very proud of your accomplishment.

3. A chance to contribute to society. Workers often see how their efforts are directly helping to bring about a more affluent, more comfortable, or more humane society. For example, workers who help meet the nation's needs for educational, social, health, and legal services know they are directly serving other human beings. Those who staff factories and offices and stores are helping to build a stronger economy. Workers who help design beautiful

This floral designer gains more than a paycheck from her job. She likes working with her hands, and finds artistic and creative pleasure in the arrangements she designs.

buildings or produce works of art have the satisfaction of uplifting human spirits and making their world more attractive.

4. Feelings of mastery and achievement. Most of us enjoy having skills. We like being good cooks or piano players, for example, and we tend to take pride in the fruits of the activities we have mastered. Throughout your work life, you can gain repeated satisfaction from learning new skills, as well as from the products or services you create with those skills.

5. Social contact. Most human beings have a strong need for give-and-take with others, and the daily people-to-people contact offered in many jobs can help workers satisfy this need. Besides leading to satisfying business relationships, the common job interests and goals developed by people who work together often lead to long-lived friendships—and sometimes marriages—as well.

6. Recognition. Don't you like to be praised and rewarded for doing a good job? Work offers numerous sources of such recognition—raises, promotions, by-lines, company or industry awards, citations, articles in employee newsletters, respect from other people in the field, and many more.

7. Mental stimulation. Girls who enjoy mental challenge, stimulation, and excitement will find abundant opportunities for these in the world of work. Consider, for example, the challenges of defending a person accused of a crime; figuring out how to cut down the paperwork that threatens to cripple a business operation; gathering facts and writing a newspaper or magazine article about a subject that really interests you; helping to make a new scientific or medical discovery; trying to find ways of helping a child overcome a physical or emotional handicap; planning an advertising campaign; or helping to plan a new city.

Private companies, government agencies, schools, and other employers need workers who can do research, solve problems, teach, analyze information, invent new products or processes, and do countless other tasks demanding intelligence and imagination. If you enjoy using your mind, you can find a lifetime of pleasure in such tasks.

8. A chance to compete. Ours is a competitive society, and women as well as men may develop strong urges to do battle and win. A working woman can satisfy her competitive needs by trying to win prizes or promotions, trying to outdo her own last accomplishment, outselling competing firms, or helping to make her office, company, or organization tops in its field.

9. A sense of identity. Ask the woman who does not work outside the home, "Who are you?" and she is apt to say, "I am Ann Brown. I am John Brown's wife and Jim and Judy Brown's mother." In other words, she describes herself in terms of her family, not as a person who has accomplished things in her own right. Work can help you to build an identity based on your own actions and achievements, as well as on your family relationships. Men have long seen themselves as workers, fathers, and husbands. Women can achieve and enjoy the same kind of three-pronged identity.

All told, the world of work offers so many possible satisfactions that no girl need dread the prospect of spending twenty-five years or more on the job. Indeed, work can be an activity you look forward to! Not all work is rewarding, however; some jobs are noisy, dirty, dangerous, poorly paid, boring, exhausting, or represent a dead end. Others are unsatisfying because they do not meet a worker's unique needs.

Long-Term Career Planning

To reap as much enjoyment as possible from work, you need to make career plans based on your own likes and dislikes, your personal and professional goals, your abilities, and the realities of the workplace. You need to look ahead and chart a career course likely to offer maximum rewards at every stage of your work life, from first job to retirement.

Long-range career planning is more difficult for women than it is for men because women's work patterns are so much more irregular than men's. Most high-school boys can safely assume that they will be in the work force, probably continuously, from the time they start working until they reach retirement age. No matter whether they marry at age 18 or age 38, no matter whether they have four children or none, no matter when they become fathers, and no matter what their wives' occupations, most will work, with little chance of interruption, for about forty-five years.

Women's work patterns, on the other hand, are very closely tied to their personal life decisions. As the statistics show, women's careers are usually interrupted by child-rearing responsibilities. Furthermore, a woman's work decisions may be influenced by her husband's earning capacity, his job, his opinions about women and work, and the longevity of their marriage. The wife whose spouse is offered a handsome promotion—if he moves to a different location—may find herself giving up her own job and looking for whatever employment is available near her new home.

Such factors create obstacles to long-range career planning but make long-term planning essential. By anticipating the possibility of being out of the work force while your children are young, or of wanting to work part time while they are in school, or of deciding to move wherever your husband's job takes him, you can prepare in advance for such events. If you want to have children, for example, you might decide to train for an occupation that will be easy to reenter when they are in school. You might also prepare for a job that offers many part-time job opportunities or is in demand in every part of the country. Seeing the possibility that you may need to work at any stage of your life, you might also plan to learn job skills that are apt to be needed for many years to come. By taking such steps, you can increase your chances of enjoying to the fullest every stage of your work life.

Although they should be long-term, your career plans should also be flexible enough to allow for the changes that are bound to occur within yourself and in the work world over time. Girls who make hard-and-fast career decisions too early may find themselves training for a highly specialized occupation that does not really interest them or lacking school courses they need to get into a particular type of education or training program. Besides, many girls do not know until they have had some employment experience what type of work might suit them best. Just as a sailor steers a zigzag course toward a destination, you may have to explore various jobs or employment arrangements before determining what you enjoy most. This does not mean you should drift along without some kind of goal in mind, however.

As an old Chinese adage says, "A journey of a thousand miles starts with a single step." Girls taking the first step toward their work lives need at least to decide in which general direction to travel. To make that decision, you need to learn as much as you can about yourself and the world of work.

References

Ghozeil, Sue, "Staff and Distaff: Why Women Work," *Manpower,* U.S. Department of Labor, Manpower Administration, December 1973.

State of California, Advisory Commission on the Status of Women, *Counseling California Girls,* 1973.

Stevenson, Gloria, "Career Planning for High School Girls," *Occupational Outlook Quarterly,* U.S. Department of Labor, Bureau of Labor Statistics, Summer 1973.

U.S. Department of Labor, Women's Bureau, *Handbook on Women Workers,* 1969.

CHAPTER II

Learn About Yourself

Suppose you could plan a dream vacation. Forget such limits as cost and time and distance, and pretend you can go anywhere in the world and do anything that you want. How would you decide what kind of vacation to take? Probably by figuring out how and where you could have the best time. This is exactly the same tack to take when planning a career.

This approach may surprise some of you, particularly those who think the word "work" conflicts with the words "a good time." But having a good time means doing something you are interested in and enjoy, and that is precisely what you hope to be doing at work. Aim for work that is so enjoyable you would do it even if you were not being paid, work that is so absorbing and interesting that you will not think of watching the clock or calling in "sick" when you are not. No job is perfect, of course; all work has its times of frustration, monotony, or drudgery. But set your sights on work offering rewards and satisfactions much beyond its disadvantages. The more job satisfaction you aim for, the more you are likely to get.

The first step in planning a career that you will really enjoy is finding an occupational field that you will really enjoy. Some girls know at a very early age what kind of work they would like to do when they grow up, but many others have no idea what they might enjoy until they are in their twenties or even later. As a practical matter, it is good to have at least a tentative selection by the time you enter high school in order to select courses suitable for your field. But self-knowledge is far more important to

COURTESY U.S. DEPARTMENT OF LABOR

Knowing what you like to do is a first step toward planning a career you will enjoy. This dog lover has chosen to set up a shop in which she grooms poodles.

occupational selection than timing. Before you can determine what kind of work you might enjoy, you need to have a clear picture of your interests, talents, personality traits, values, personal goals—and also your limitations. All these factors will come into play on the job, and the better you know your own characteristics, the better equipped you will be to find work that matches them well.

Taking a Personal Inventory

One way of gaining self-knowledge is by making a personal inventory of those personal traits that will affect your stay in the world of work. When trying to clarify your own characteristics, likes, dislikes, preferences, and wants, however, try to make sure you are looking at your own traits, and not the traits your parents, boyfriend, or teachers think you have or want you to have.

Many girls, especially those who have been brought up to be "good" or to seek the approval of others and respect convention and authority, try to do what others would like them to do. They may, for example, adopt certain hobbies or activities because they are expected to. This is a mistake in career planning. You are the one who is going to be working for twenty-five years or so; you are the one who will ultimately feel happy or unhappy on the job. You are therefore the one who must assume responsibility for achieving work satisfaction. The only way to do this is by deciding who you are and what you want. Trying to do or be what someone else wants you to do or be is like trying to wear someone else's old shoes. At best, they will pinch or rub only a little. At worst, they will be impossible to walk in.

Keeping this in mind, you might begin career planning by looking at the things you really like to do. Exactly what are they?

The answers to that question—and there are bound to be many—may come from any part of your life, because practically anything you enjoy doing can be linked with some kind of job. You might start by looking at your experiences in school. Do you like to study? What courses do you enjoy? What kinds of school projects have you enjoyed most: writing papers, doing library research, conducting science experiments, building models, giving oral reports, producing a mock radio or television show, drawing or painting or working with clay, cooking, or sewing?

Your extracurricular activities probably offer other clues to the kind of work you might enjoy doing. Do you enjoy debating or participating in school plays or working on the school newspaper? Have you been involved in the school band or chorus? Do you enjoy working as a student assistant in the school library? Have you played on a basketball or softball or hockey team?

Do not forget to look at your leisure activities when taking stock of your interests, for activities that you now do for fun can lead to work you will consider fun. What do you do in your spare time: read, talk with friends, sew, collect stamps, refinish furniture? If you enjoy reading, is there a particular topic you especially like to read about? What kinds of television programs do you like to watch? If you enjoy keeping up with current events, are you most interested in politics or economics or social trends or some other area? Are you involved in a hobby such as photography? Do you enjoy driving a car, swimming or participating in other sports, or gardening? Do you like to travel? Are you involved in club activities?

Job experiences and volunteer activities offer further indications of your interests. Have you enjoyed baby-sitting or working in a restaurant, office, or store? Did you ever tutor children or do volunteer work in a hospital or home for the aged? Have you had fun working on a farm? Do you like to walk dogs or tend plants for people who are on vacation?

For career-planning purposes, knowing yourself should mean knowing both what you like to do and why you like to do these things. Different occupations and jobs offer different kinds of satisfactions, and defining the reasons you enjoy particular activities can help you choose a job field with similar rewards.

You might start by asking yourself exactly what appeals to you about a particular activity. If you like math courses, for example, what do you like about them: doing calculations, translating written problems into equations, learning and using mathematical rules and formulas, working with abstractions? If you like sewing, do you particularly enjoy working with your hands, operating the machine, creating a finished product from scratch, or saving money on clothes? You may be active in your school's student government. If you are, exactly what do you like about this activity? If you are a student assistant in the school library, do you most enjoy helping library users, keeping books and cards arranged in precise order, or simply being part of the world of books and literature?

Here is an exercise that might help you inventory both the activities you enjoy and the pleasures you get from them: jot down, as quickly as you can, twenty things that you really like to do. Do not worry if they do not seem job-related; if two of your favorite pastimes are listening to popular music and crocheting, put them down.

When you have finished, go down the list and mark each item to show whether it involves working with people (put a P beside the item), ideas (I), or things (T). Mark a C beside activities that relate to children and an O beside those you do outdoors. Decide whether you enjoy each activity alone (A) or with someone else (S). Determine whether it requires physical (Ph) or mental (M) effort—it could involve both—and whether it is something you do with your hands (H) or with tools (T).

This exercise may help you see patterns in the kinds of things you enjoy. You may find, for example, that nearly everything—or virtually nothing—you like to do involves work with your hands. This kind of knowledge is invaluable in making sound occupational choices. If you are happiest working with your hands, for example, you might well decide to choose a field that requires manual effort.

Determining Your Aptitudes

Knowing what you like to do is a big step toward choosing a satisfying career field, but there are many other considerations. For example, because it is very difficult to enjoy work that one has little talent for, a good knowledge of your aptitudes is a second essential in successful occupational choice.

An aptitude is a talent or knack for a particular kind of activity. It is the ability to learn a certain kind of skill or to acquire a specific type of knowledge. Having a strong aptitude in a particular area does not mean you have mastered skills in that area, just that you have the ability to. Different occupations require different aptitudes, and if you are to be good at a particular kind of work, you may need to have a fairly strong flair for that field.

We can generally pick out our aptitudes by looking at the things we learn easiest and best. Some girls, for example, learn math principles effortlessly. Others have a hard time with math, but can easily understand and use the rules of grammar. Others excel in athletics, but have difficulty in the classroom. Some girls easily learn skills in many areas. All these situations may reflect individual differences in aptitude.

Our interests and aptitudes often coincide. But this is not necessarily so. Consider a girl whose heart is set on being a singer but who is unable to hit the right notes even after years of singing lessons. She lacks the aptitude needed for this occupation. So does the girl who wants to be an actress but who has such a bad memory that she cannot remember a three-line part.

Following are some basic aptitudes. While going down the list, try to figure out exactly where your strongest aptitudes lie.

1. Capacity to understand and use words. Because so much learning depends on being able to understand both written materials and speech, an aptitude for grasping ideas expressed in words

is considered a large part of overall intelligence. Persons with this aptitude can generally learn to read well, follow directions easily, use words effectively, and speak well. They are likely to develop good vocabularies for both writing and speech. Writers, lawyers, teachers, secretaries, scientists, librarians, and salespeople are among workers for whom a good aptitude for words is important.

2. Capacity to use numbers and to solve mathematical problems. If your aptitude for this field is strong, you can learn to add, subtract, multiply, and divide quickly and accurately, you can easily understand relationships between numbers, and you probably get top grades in mathematics. Fields that demand good numerical skills include engineering, accounting, bookkeeping, and sales work.

3. Reasoning. People with a good capacity for reasoning understand overall concepts and can see how things fit or do not fit together. They can figure things out, solve problems on the basis of their past experience, and effectively plan ahead. Executives, lawyers, doctors, and scientists are among workers to whom reasoning ability is very important. However, most jobs—and life in general—require some reasoning aptitude.

4. The capacity for visualizing relationships between objects in space. Engineers, architects, and artists are among those who need a knack for picturing forms and imagining how they will look or work together. If you are good at geometry or can do jigsaw puzzles quickly, you probably possess this ability.

5. Finger dexterity. This is the ability to use your fingers to move small articles or tools rapidly and accurately. Crocheting and embroidering require finger dexterity, as do typing, repairing jewelry or watches, and assembling electronics components or other small factory-made items.

6. Manual dexterity. People with manual dexterity can use their hands to manipulate tools and other objects quickly and

precisely. This ability is needed in sewing, making pottery, refinishing furniture, and dressing a baby. Carpenters, doctors and nurses, automobile mechanics, and others who work with their hands generally need manual dexterity.

7. An ear for music. This aptitude enables one to understand musical forms and learn to play musical instruments easily. It is vital for people who want to become musical performers.

8. Color discrimination. An eye for color and the ability to combine colors effectively are essential for artists, designers, and interior decorators. A flair in this direction often appears in a girl's knack for choosing clothes in becoming colors or decorating her room attractively.

9. Clerical capacity. This is the talent for seeing differences and mistakes in written materials. It is very important to workers such as secretaries, proofreaders, and editors. If you often spot typographical errors in the newspaper, if misspelled words tend to jump out of reading material and glare at you, you probably have a strong clerical bent.

10. Memory. People with good memories are able to recall details, numbers, names, and other facts. Not everybody with a good aptitude for remembering remembers the same kinds of things, however; some people are particularly good at telephone numbers, others remember names, and others never forget a face. Secretaries, accountants, librarians, politicians, and many other workers need good memories.

11. Coordination of hands and eyes. People whose hands and eyes work well together usually can learn to hit a moving ball with a bat or racquet. Those without this aptitude often wind up swinging at the air. Good eye-hand coordination is very important for artists, architects, and workers in craft and repair jobs.

Knowing exactly what your talents are can help you be realistic in choosing a career field. You can avoid the unhappiness and frustration of picking an occupation that is discouragingly hard—or even impossible—for you to master, and instead choose one that matches your natural talents. The more flair you have for the field you choose, the happier and more successful you are likely to be.

But having a particular aptitude does not necessarily mean you should pursue an occupation that requires it. Your chosen field must also suit your personality. The woman who is naturally shy and reserved would probably hate a sales job where she has to approach strangers and try to convince them to buy her product. On the other hand, the sociable and outgoing woman may love this kind of work but detest a research job where she would be working by herself all day.

Examining Your Character Traits

It is often hard for people to assess their own personalities realistically, but a clear picture of your personal traits is an immense help in occupational selection. You might get a fix on some aspects of your own personality by answering the following questions: Are you loyal to your family and friends? Do you genuinely enjoy other people? Are you warm and friendly? Are you shy? Do you flare up in anger easily? Do you have a sense of responsibility? Do you look and plan ahead? Do you see things that need to be done and take the initiative for doing them, or do you wait for directions from others? Do you make things happen in your life, or do you wait and let things happen to you? Are you honest? Do you accept other people's points of view, even if you don't agree with them? Can you tolerate differences of opinion, or do such differences disturb you? Are you outspoken about your opinions? Do you control your emotions? Do you have a sense of humor?

Your work habits are an important part of your personality, and a good understanding of them is another boon in wise career planning. Do you tend to wait until the last minute to study for exams or write papers? If you do, you will most likely be happier in a job where there is pressure from periodic task deadlines rather than in one that demands a constant level of day-to-day effort. On the other hand, if you freeze under pressure, you may be best off avoiding occupations riddled with frequent crises or emergencies.

Do you like to do the same kind of work—say solving one type of math problem—over and over, or do you become bored with repetition and prefer more variety in work? Would you rather come up with ideas or carry them through? Many people are outstanding in one and washouts in the other. Would you prefer to give orders or take them? Do you like to do detail work or work that requires extreme accuracy? Do you do your best work at a particular time of the day—morning, for example? If so, you might want to try to select an occupation whose work hours match or can be adapted to your body's schedule. Do you like to work on one long-term project at a time, or do you enjoy switching from project to project frequently? Do you like to see a tangible finished project when you have completed a work project? If so, you may feel dissatisfied in jobs that do not provide concrete evidence of your efforts.

Following are some personality and character traits that will influence your actions in the world of work. Can you pick out the ones that apply to you?

Adventurous	Calm	Competitive
Ambitious	Careful	Confident
Assertive	Careless	Conscientious
Bold	Cheerful	Cooperative
Broad-minded	Clear-thinking	Creative

Crisis-oriented	Lazy	Reliable
Curious	Leisurely	Reserved
Dependable	Logical	Scholarly
Determined	Loyal	Self-confident
Disorganized	Methodical	Sensible
Easy-going	Meticulous	Serious
Enterprising	Neat	Shy
Enthusiastic	Nervous	Sociable
Ethical	Orderly	Stable
Explosive	Organized	Strong-minded
Flexible	Outgoing	Sympathetic
Friendly	Patient	Tactful
Good-natured	Persevering	Teachable
Hard-working	Practical	Thorough
Helpful	Precise	Thoughtful
Honest	Procrastinating	Tolerant
Imaginative	Punctual	Trustworthy
Impatient	Quick	Understanding
Independent	Quick-tempered	Unexcitable
Intelligent	Quiet	Versatile
Introverted	Realistic	Witty

Recognizing Your Values

Besides knowing your own interests, talents, and personal traits, you also need a good fix on your values if you want to make wise career decisions. Your values are your ideas and feelings about what is right, wrong, good, bad, important, and unimportant. Such judgments will play a large role in determining both the personal and work-related goals you set for yourself.

As a beginning point for clarifying your values, try figuring out which of the following are most important to you:

Getting married
Being a good mother
Being well-liked
Having lots of money
Doing things you enjoy doing
Having good health
Living up to your moral standards
Becoming famous
Having power over others
Getting recognition
Helping others
Being independent

The relative importance you place on each of these could determine your happiness or unhappiness in different types of work. For example, if you feel that misrepresenting the facts—even a tiny bit—is wrong, you should probably stay away from fields in which facts are shaded every day in order to make a point or a sale. If you believe your work should be useful to society or should help or serve others, look for a field in which you will feel you are contributing to the well-being of your fellow humans. If you have any strong notions that certain activities or practices are morally wrong, take these into account. Imagine how difficult it would be for a woman who strongly opposes environmental pollution, for example, to work in an industry that steadily spews tons of wastes into the air or nearby waters.

Look also at the rewards of employment that are important to you. Is it important that your job offer you the chance to make a great deal of money or to gain prestige, fame, power, or social standing? If you value any of these, you may feel dissatisfied in a field that does not offer opportunities for such rewards. Do not make the mistake of choosing a particular field primarily because of such external rewards, however. All the power, prestige, fame, or money in the world is apt to be meaningless and unsatisfying if you have to do work you dislike or morally oppose. Besides, if you enjoy an activity and have the aptitude to do it well, you will probably succeed in work based on that activity. When that happens, such benefits as money and prestige or renown could well come along.

Your values concerning the relative importance of work, marriage, and motherhood in your life are especially important in career planning. When examining these, try to distinguish your own values—those based on your own personal experiences, feelings, and preferences—from those reflecting society's general expectations for women. A close examination of your beliefs may show that your values are different from those traditionally accepted by women. For example, you, like a growing number of women and girls, may disagree with the following values, all of which are widely held in our society.

Women who remain single or childless are "failures."

A wife's job should be secondary to her wifely and domestic duties. If these conflict, she should give up her job.

Women who work outside the home when their children are young are bad mothers.

Women who are seriously interested in careers are "unfeminine" or unattractive.

Working women who try to achieve power, fame, or wealth are too aggressive.

Your career plans should take into account your values concerning marriage, work, and children. If you want to have children, for example, and if you feel it is important for a mother to stay home full time with pre-school-age children, you probably will decide to quit work entirely while your children are young. You might then do well to choose a career field in which it will be relatively easy to keep up with technological or procedural changes that occur in the occupation while you are out of the work force. You might also make sure that the field you select will be relatively easy to reenter if you want to return to work later.

On the other hand, if you want children but believe it important to your own happiness to continue working, at least part time, while they are young, you might want to make sure that opportunities for part-time work are abundant in any field you prepare for. You might also consider the possibility of working full time and paying someone else to care for your children or clean your home or both. If this is your preference, you should remember that paying for such services will take a big bite out of your income and select an occupation that will pay you enough to afford to hire competent help.

Look, too, at the relative importance you place on work and family responsibilities. If you feel strongly that your work duties should not cut into time you want to spend with your family, you may want to avoid occupations in which you may have to work evenings and weekends, when your family is likely to be at home.

Considering Physical Limitations and Assets

A sure knowledge of your interests, talents, personality traits, values, and personal goals will give you a firm foundation for choosing a work field you are apt to find satisfying. To avoid needless disappointment in career planning, however, another bit of self-knowledge is needed: a good awareness of any physical limitations that might prevent you from entering or doing well at fields you would otherwise enjoy.

General poor health is one such limitation. Good health is an asset to all workers, of course; it is hard to enjoy any activity or perform it well if one does not feel up to par.

You should also keep in mind any physical characteristics that

The job of tour guide may appeal to girls who enjoy traveling, working directly with people, being outdoors, and paying attention to details. Girls planning careers need to become aware of such personal preferences.

might hinder your effectiveness in particular fields. For example, some workers must have the stamina to spend long hours on their feet. If you lack such stamina, you may have difficulty working as a beautician, department-store buyer or salesclerk, dentist or dental assistant, or surgeon. Are you unusually short, tall, fat, or thin? If so, you may not be able to meet height and weight specifications often set for stewardesses, policewomen, and women in the armed services. If you are interested in such occupations as carpentry and automobile repair, make sure you have the physical strength these jobs demand. Good eyesight is important in many fields, and girls with visual defects should have them corrected and carefully check vision requirements in any fields they consider.

Some physical characteristics are assets in the work world, and it does not hurt to keep these in mind when you are assessing your physical traits. Strength and stamina are advantages for women who want to enter the skilled trades, for example, and many employers seek women with attractive faces and figures for jobs that require much public contact—airline jobs, public-relations slots, and receptionist positions, for example.

Obtaining an Outside Opinion

Once you have examined your interests, talents, personality traits, values, personal goals, and physical limitations, you may have a pretty good notion of who you are, what you like, what you can do, and what you want out of life. On the other hand, you may still feel you have large gaps in your self-knowledge. Perhaps you are not sure what really interests you, or where your talents lie, or what your personal goals are. In this case, it might be smart to get an outside opinion that will help you double-check the accuracy of your self-assessment or fill in any blanks. School counselors can often provide such extra help.

Based on his or her past dealings with you, your school guidance or vocational counselor may be aware of certain talents or traits you do not realize you have. The counselor may also be able to help by supplying additional information from your school records—teachers' evaluations concerning your strengths and weaknesses in the classroom, for example. Moreover, school counselors can often administer or tell you where to take various kinds of tests that may add to your knowledge of yourself. Such tests can help verify information you already have or lead you to new self-understanding.

Several kinds of tests are available. Vocational interest tests such as the Kuder Preference Record are designed to help pinpoint the activities that interest you. The Kuder test shows, for example, whether you like to work outdoors, do mechanical work, work with numbers, do clerical work, analyze problems, or meet people and persuade them to do something. It also shows whether you are interested in art, literature, or music, and whether you want work that enables you to help people.

Another vocational interest test is the Strong Vocational Interest Blank (SVIB). By comparing your interests with those of people who have succeeded in a variety of different occupations, this test may help you see which fields you might enjoy. This test was originally designed for men. A special form of SVIB has been developed for women but has limits which prompt some counselors to recommend that girls taking the SVIB complete both forms. An SVIB form that merges the men's and women's versions was developed recently but is untested.

Other tests can help you zero in on your aptitudes. Among these are tests that measure your scholastic aptitude—often called "intelligence"—or your mental abilities. Others test physical as well as mental aptitudes. For example, the General Aptitude Test Battery developed by the U.S. Employment Service tests your talents in areas such as arithmetic reasoning, finger dexterity, computation, clerical ability, ability to recognize and match various shapes, and ability to comprehend three-dimensional forms. The test is available to counselors who want to administer it to school students.

Personality inventories may also help you gain a clearer idea of your personality traits. Some of these are designed to measure emotional stability and personal adjustment. Others list typical problems faced by young people within certain age groups. Pinpointing the problems that concern you and talking these over with your counselor may give you a clearer idea of your personality traits.

Remember, however, that no test is perfectly accurate. Testing is not an exact science, and human characteristics are far too complex to be neatly summed up in standardized test results. Moreover, many guidance tests currently in use have been developed for or are based on information obtained from men or boys and may not be as useful for females as they are for males. This means that girls need to be especially careful to evaluate test results critically. Nevertheless, tests administered and interpreted properly can help point the way to much new information about yourself.

A thorough self-inventory, sessions with your school counselor, and possibly talks with friends or family members who know you well should help you gain the kind of self-knowledge you need to choose an occupational field wisely. (Incidentally, there are probably several fields in which you could be happy, just as there are probably several houses you would enjoy living in or several men you could like being married to. Girls who fail to realize this may agonize unnecessarily over occupational decisions, because they are frightened that they may not pick the "right" field.)

How will you know when you have gathered enough information about yourself to make sound career plans? Chances are you will feel that you have a pretty good—but not perfect—idea of who you are and what you want. Don't be discouraged if this feeling doesn't come immediately. For many people, getting to know themselves is a difficult, slow process.

Effects of Personal Change

Even if you do develop a clear picture of yourself fairly quickly, that picture will need to be touched up now and then to take into account the changes you will undergo during your lifetime. As you gain new experiences through work, travel, school, community activities, marriage, motherhood, or the many other things you may do in your lifetime, you will develop new interests and discover new abilities. Your values and goals are also likely to change. If your initial occupational decisions are based on solid self-understanding, you should, unless you change radically, be able to make career adjustments that will keep your work life in line with the changes that will influence your satisfaction on the job. 1999732

Besides keeping up with natural changes, you might want to work at changing certain features in your self-portrait that may hinder your attempts to find satisfaction in the work world. Suppose, for example, that you have difficulty deciding what really interests you, or that you feel you have no real interests. The problem may be that your experiences have never brought you into contact with some activities you might thoroughly enjoy.

As boys and girls grow up, they are channeled into activities that society sees as appropriate for that sex. You may have been given dolls and a miniature baking set to play with when you were little, whereas your brother got cars and trucks and building sets. You may have gone shopping with your mother while your brother went fishing with Dad. Maybe you took cooking and sewing lessons in junior high or high school and the boys in your class learned woodworking and mechanical drawing. Inasmuch as you don't know whether you like doing something until you try it, you might want to make a point of exploring some of the activities that you have never tried simply because you are a girl.

You might try to build a wooden cabinet or a model ship, or learn to repair a bicycle or toaster. By exploring such "boys' " fields, you may develop interests and discover talents you never suspected you had.

Your previous experiences may have also been limited by the area of the country in which you live, your parents' income level, your family's interests, and other factors. In the interests of promoting your own happiness, you might try to find ways to broaden your experience and knowledge of new fields.

You may also want to try to change any personality traits or work habits that could stand in the way of your happiness and effectiveness on the job. Certain traits can enhance your performance and enjoyment in just about any type of work. These include: self-confidence; a good sense of humor; ability to get along well with others; dependability; courage to stand up for ideas you strongly believe in, even in the face of opposition; independence; willingness to set work-related goals and to do what you must to overcome obstacles and achieve them; ability to follow through on an idea or carry a work project to its completion; and willingness to accept responsibility for your own actions and decisions instead of passing the buck.

On the other hand, some characteristics can hurt you in just about any job: a bad temper; inability to get along well with people; shyness that interferes with your ability to speak up for yourself, to ask people for information you need, or to deal with people in positions of authority; inability to accept criticism; constant fear of failure or unwillingness to accept new challenges or responsibilities; inability to concentrate; and being so upset by your own mistakes that you cannot admit your errors and go back to work.

Girls who suffer feelings like these need to learn to like themselves more. They need to learn that they are worthwhile human beings who, like all other human beings, have both strengths and weaknesses. One way to work at achieving this feeling is by recognizing your good points and achievements. Take credit for your accomplishments, no matter what they are, without downgrading them. You are unique, and because no one else has your unique qualities, you cannot measure your worth against others'. Instead, concentrate on your own strengths and talents, and develop them to their fullest.

Girls with low self-esteem also need to stop criticizing themselves for their mistakes and to look at these as human errors to try to grow beyond. Girls who can do this are apt to gain confidence and trust in themselves. These feelings, in turn, strengthen a girl's ability to get along with people, overcome shyness, and feel the courage to take on and succeed at work projects or goals.

If you need help in overcoming a poor self-image or in developing the kinds of traits that will make you a happier and more effective person, do not hestitate to consult a school counselor. Other persons and agencies who offer such help, usually for a fee, are listed in the *Directory of Counseling Services,* published every year by the American Personnel and Guidance Association. Write to this association at 1607 New Hampshire Avenue, N.W., Washington, D.C. 20036 for information about buying the booklet.

References

Catalyst, *Planning for Work,* New York City, 1973.

Gibson, Robert L. and Robert E. Higgins, *Techniques of Guidance: An Approach to Pupil Analysis,* Science Research Associates, Inc., Chicago, 1966.

Kimbell, Grady and Ben S. Vineyard, *Succeeding in the World of Work,* McKnight & McKnight Publishing Co., Bloomington, Illinois, 1970.

Kiplinger Washington Editors, Inc., *You, Your Job & Your Future,* Washington, D.C., 1964.

U.S. Department of Labor, Bureau of Employment Security, *Choosing Your Occupation,* 1965.

CHAPTER III

Investigating Occupations

Learning about yourself is a little like putting together a jigsaw puzzle: you turn over bits and pieces of self-knowledge and fit them together to form a picture, a self-portrait. Learning about the world of work, the second stage of career planning, is more like being a detective; you need to investigate different occupations thoroughly and gather specific clues that will help you figure out what kind of work you might like best.

Girls who actively and systematically investigate the work world are apt to collect more and better information than girls who gather fragments of occupational knowledge through such chance events as meeting someone in a field that sounds appealing or happening upon a magazine article about workers in a certain field.

If you already have an occupation or two in mind, you need to explore thoroughly the realities of work in those fields, as well as in related occupations that you might enjoy. If you are groping for a field to enter, start by investigating work related to your stronger interests and talents. If those do not seem suitable, look into fields that mesh with some of your other abilities and preferences. A good look at both yourself and the job world is bound to turn up at least one occupational area—and will probably yield several—that will satisfy at least a few of your interests and needs. This could be the beginning of a career you custom-tailor to suit other parts of your personality as well.

During the initial stage of occupational exploration, a useful strategy is to learn as much as you can about occupations in which work activities or subject areas that interest you are central. If biology is your favorite school subject, look into fields based on a knowledge of the biological sciences. Examples are biologist, professional health occupations, conservation occupations, biology teacher, technician occupations that involve the biological sciences, technical writer in the field of biology, and a host of others.

You might also explore occupations that share a type of work activity for which you have a bent, say, sales jobs, writing occupations, driving occupations, craft and repair work, or teaching occupations. Another approach to exploring related occupations is to look at work done within the various segments of our economy—recreation, health care, transportation, banking, construction, education, business, entertainment, government, religion, land use, or any other field that interests you.

The U.S. Office of Education has developed fifteen "career clusters" that may be used as guidelines to exploring closely linked occupations. These clusters are business and office occupations, marketing and distribution occupations, communications and media occupations, construction occupations, manufacturing occupations, transportation occupations, agribusiness and natural resources occupations, marine science occupations, environmental control occupations, public services occupations, health occupations, hospitality and recreation occupations, personal services occupations, fine arts and humanities occupations, and consumer and homemaking-related occupations.

Exploring occupational groups rather than single occupations gives you a broader perspective on the job world. You learn more about the different kinds of work available than you would by looking into only one field or a few unrelated occupations. Learning about the nature of the work, educational requirements, benefits and shortcoming of each of a cluster of related occupations also gives you a basis for comparing several fields that might appeal to you and choosing the one that seems best suited to your needs.

Exploring closely linked occupational fields may also open your eyes to a variety of jobs you might not otherwise consider. Suppose, for example, that you like working with numbers. If you immediately think of becoming a bookkeeper and explore only this occupation, you may never think of becoming an accountant, statistician, mathematician, or statistical clerk. Yet, one of these math-related jobs might suit your abilities, interests, and temperament better than the occupation of bookkeeper—and may offer better income and job prospects, too.

The knowledge you gain from exploring groups of occupations also gives you an extra measure of job versatility. Should you ever find yourself dissatisfied with an occupation you choose and prepare for, you will have some ideas about related jobs to which you might switch. The same holds true if your occupation becomes obsolete because of technological change (an event that it is hoped you will foresee if you explore the field thoroughly) or if job openings become scarce. A knowledge of related occupations will give you some idea of other fields you might easily move into.

Aspects of Various Employment Fields

When investigating any occupation, you need to gather a variety of facts.

1. The nature of the work. Before you can wisely decide

whether you might enjoy an occupation, you have to find out exactly what workers in that field do. It is not enough to think vaguely that psychologists "help the emotionally disturbed" or that interior decorators "decorate homes." Workers perform these broad functions by doing specific physical or mental tasks that require particular kinds of knowledge, skills, and tools. You have to learn exactly what these are when exploring any field.

To judge whether or not an occupation would suit your personality and value system, you also need to find out if workers in the occupation do one kind of task over and over or if they perform a variety of duties. Determine, too, how much creativity, initiative, and judgment the work requires, and how it contributes to society or meshes with work in other fields.

Check to see if workers usually work independently or under close supervision. Do they work alone, as members of a group, or as group leaders? These factors could all significantly affect your chances of enjoying any field.

2. Work settings. Workers may be employed in carpeted, attractively furnished offices where music plays in the background; noisy factories with dirty walls and rest rooms; large institutional kitchens where gleaming stoves are topped by huge kettles; hushed hospitals or laboratories filled with medical or scientific paraphernalia; or countless other settings. Because you will spend a great many of your waking hours on the job during the years you are employed, you should find out about the surroundings you are apt to work in.

It is important to see if any health or safety hazards are associated with the work setting. Federal and state laws require that many such hazards be eliminated or minimized, but some occupations nevertheless offer many chances for falls, machine-related mishaps, and other accidents.

You might also find out if the field offers job openings nationwide and in both urban and rural areas. Most fields do, but locations of job openings in some occupations are somewhat limited. For example, department store buyers are more apt to work in cities or suburbs than in rural areas, while motion-picture industry workers are employed primarily in New York and California. Also find out whether the field requires extensive or frequent travel.

Your colleagues will form an integral part of any work setting you enter, so find out the age and sex of workers in the occupation. Most workers must interact with co-workers while on the job, and many become friends with, date, or even marry people they meet through work. If relatively few—or nearly all—of the workers in an occupation are women, decide whether you would enjoy, dislike, or be indifferent to the situation. Find out, too, if workers deal mostly with others in the same occupation or if they have frequent contact with persons in different fields.

3. Entry requirements. You may need to go through college, graduate school, an apprenticeship program, business school, or some other kind of educational or training program in order to qualify for an occupation. You may also need a license or certificate in order to practice in the field, and you may have to pass a written examination or demonstrate your skill in the field to earn such credentials. Professional health workers and beauticians are among workers who need to meet such requirements. Workers in some fields may need to join union or professional organizations. It is to your advantage to find out how one joins such organizations, whether membership in them is limited or restricted, and what the benefits and costs of such membership are. You should also know whether workers need to pass physical or eye examinations before they can enter the field and what such examinations entail.

4. Work hours and schedules. Girls planning to combine

housework, children, and jobs should make special efforts to find
out whether occupations they explore offer many part-time job
opportunities or require workers to work weekends or evenings,
put in irregular shifts, or work for unusually long stints. Find out
whether much overtime work is available—some workers can
choose to work beyond their regular workdays or workweeks in
order to earn more money—or if overtime work may be required
in order to meet deadlines, fill rush orders, or deal with other
emergencies.

5. Personal qualifications. Having discovered your own abilities and personality traits, you now need to learn what personal
characteristics are needed to enjoy or succeed in any field you
investigate. Do not forget to find out whether workers in the field
must meet any physical requirement such as height or weight
specifications.

6. The pay. Because money is one of the rewards of all work,
it makes sense to learn how and how much workers in a given
field are paid. Do they receive annual salaries, hourly wages,
wages plus customers' tips, or sales commissions (a proportion of
the dollar amount that they sell), or are they paid according to
the amount they produce? Find out, too, how earnings compare
with those in other fields; such a comparison might prompt you
to forego some fields for others requiring the same amount of
education and training and offering work you might enjoy equally
well.

Find out how much beginning workers in the occupation make,
as well as the amount earned by workers with several years' experience, and by those in top positions within the field. You might
also check to see if earnings in the field vary significantly from
one part of the country to another. Try to collect data about
earnings in geographic areas where you prefer to work. If the
occupation offers side benefits such as free goods or services pro-

COURTESY U.S. DEPARTMENT OF LABOR

Women who want to become police officers may need to meet height, weight, age, and educational requirements and be in excellent health. Finding out about job requirements is a vital part of occupational investigation.

duced in the field or free or inexpensive travel, think of these as extra income.

7. Personal rewards of the work. Check to see whether a field offers workers the chance to take responsibility for their own decisions or actions, contribute meaningfully to society, help others, gain recognition, follow projects through to their completion,

or enjoy other personal rewards. Does it allow workers to use their creative talents or take pride in the products they make or services they render? Obtaining this kind of information will enable you to see how an occupation meshes with your own values concerning work.

8. Advancement possibilities. Some occupations offer workers very few chances to earn more money, take on increased or more challenging responsibilities, or learn new skills. Such limitations are most likely to occur in occupations requiring the least amount of education or training. Waitresses with twenty years' experience, for example, may earn little more or do little more than beginners. On the other hand, many fields offer good opportunities for advancement, including the chance to be promoted to supervisory positions.

Find out how far up the ladder workers can move. What are the top positions open to secretaries, for example, or secondary-school teachers? Exactly what do workers in top slots do and how much do they earn? Find out also whether workers need additional education or training to move from entry-level jobs to higher positions and whether employers in the field offer or will help pay for such training.

Because you will be a working *woman,* you might want to look carefully at the record of women's advancement in fields you explore. This will be especially important to girls who enjoy performing well and being recognized for their achievements. Are capable women given increased responsibilities and promotions? How many women hold top jobs in the field? The absence of a significant number of women in top-level positions need not discourage ambitious girls from entering an occupation, but it does indicate that they may need to work especially hard to overcome previous promotion patterns.

9. The employment outlook. Girls who choose an occupation

without finding out how good or bad its job prospects are likely to be when they join the work force are foolish. Preparing for an occupation generally means investing time and energy—and perhaps money—in training. Smart girls find out in advance if such investments are likely to pay off in job opportunities.

Job prospects in any occupation change over time. Employment grows or dwindles, and the field may even become obsolete. Sometimes occupations face shortages of skilled workers, and sometimes the number of trained job hunters outstrips the number of available jobs. Girls planning careers need to find out which of these situations are most likely to prevail when they are ready to look for work.

Be wary of fields in which employment is declining. Such fields may be on the way to extinction. You have to decide for yourself whether to risk preparing for fields in which the supply of workers is expected to exceed the number of openings, however. If the occupation is one for which you have an especially strong talent or one that you very much want to enter, you may elect to prepare for it despite the employment outlook, perhaps thinking that you are likely to excel in the field and will therefore have a good chance of finding work even if job competition is keen. On the other hand, you may not be willing to gamble. In many of the so-called "glamour" occupations—modeling and jobs in the performing arts, for example—job prospects are relatively poor because the number of people looking for work is much greater than the number of jobs. Girls considering these fields will probably need to be very talented, extremely well qualified, or downright lucky in order to find work.

Like the number of job openings, the nature of work in any occupation may change over time, often because of new technological developments. Workers in fields in which new machines or equipment are frequently introduced may need to update their skills or learn new ones often in order to keep pace. Women who leave such occupations for several years may find that their skills become obsolete while they are out of the work force. It is therefore crucial that if you are planning to interrupt work to raise children you learn what impact technology is likely to have on the occupation in future years. Computer programming and operating are among fields whose work may change substantially in the future as a result of changing technology. Girls considering these fields should consider the consequences of such changes.

When exploring future job prospects, consider, too, that the number of opportunities within any occupation varies widely from industry to industry. To cite one clerical example, bank tellers are employed only in the banking industry, but bookkeepers are needed in virtually every sector of the economy. In the interests of keeping your future employment horizons as open as possible, you may want to avoid occupations in which job opportunities are limited to only a few industries.

10. Related occupations. Many jobs provide training and experience that enable workers to succeed in other occupations. A doctor or nurse, for example, might be able to move into hospital administration; and an engineer might turn to selling engineering products, designing equipment or machinery, writing technical materials, or doing public-relations work for an engineering firm. Finding out what opportunities for lateral career occupational changes are possible in fields you explore may help you decide whether or not you want to enter a field.

11. Impact of the field on workers' off-the-job activities. The occupation you choose could have a great impact on your lifestyle. By determining your income, it will help to determine the kind of house or apartment you can afford, the kind of clothes you wear, and your social status. Your field could influence your political views and determine the kind of books and magazines

you read. It might also shape your overall values and attitudes about life.

An occupation can also require specific off-the-job behavior. For example, public-relations and sales workers may need to attend social gatherings or entertain out-of-town visitors or clients during evenings or weekends. Similarly, the social, civic, and recreational activities of teachers may be influenced—and are sometimes restricted—by customs and attitudes in their communities. Girls who choose such fields should be prepared to behave as required.

Characteristics of Occupational Information

The easiest, most practical, and most widely used way to learn such facts about occupations is through published information. However, published materials, and these include audiovisual aids and information available through computers as well as written materials, share certain limitations, many of which stem from the inherent difficulties of describing occupations accurately and without distortion.

In the first place, working conditions within an occupation often vary tremendously from one employer to another or from one part of the country to another. The job duties, educational requirements, pay, and advancement potential of a librarian working in a small public library in the rural Midwest, for example, are apt to be very different from those of a librarian employed in one of the many departments within the Library of Congress in Washington, D.C. Occupational information simply cannot cover all the variations possible in working conditions within a field. Instead, published materials describe the major duties which librarians "may," "often," or "usually" perform. The result is often a very generalized, very abstract description of the occupation. Trying to learn about an occupation through this kind of description is like trying to figure out what a person looks like by studying only his or her silhouette. You can learn some important facts—the person's overall size and shape, for example—but will miss details like the color of his or her eyes.

Moreover, the job information presented in published materials has been gathered, analyzed, and written or produced by one or several people. This makes it subject to the slight distortions that occur whenever human beings try to describe reality. More important, it makes job information vulnerable to distortions by publishers who, for their own reasons, want to paint biased pictures of occupational fields. Such publishers might include companies recruiting people for certain occupations, schools that offer training in the occupations they describe, and professional or employee groups trying to create favorable public images of their fields.

Slanted occupational information often emphasizes or exaggerates the opportunities and benefits available within a field while ignoring its disadvantages or hazards. An example would be material that glowingly describes the glamour and travel benefits of being an airline stewardess but neglects to explain that stewardesses spend much of their time in repetitive, waitress-like work, work irregular hours and shifts, and may suffer "jet lag"—physical ailments associated with crossing time zones—or feelings of homelessness, uprootedness, or loneliness resulting from constant travel.

Furthermore, because the national economy and its jobs are constantly changing, career information tends to become outdated very quickly. Job duties, educational requirements, and technology change frequently even in relatively stable occupations. Published information may therefore be a bit behind the times even as it comes off the presses.

A further problem with occupational materials is that their assessments of future employment prospects are "iffy." The federal government, state government agencies, and private groups project the number of job openings likely to arise in a wide variety of occupations during the next, say, five or ten years. These projections are based on certain assumptions about future economic and social developments in the country, and, in the case of state or area projections, in a given geographic region. It may be assumed, for example, that the nation's work force will grow at a predicted rate during the years covered by the projections, that employment and unemployment rates will continue at prior levels, and the nation's social and educational patterns will not change drastically. If these assumptions are unjustified, or if a major economic or social development—a recession or war, perhaps—unexpectedly occurs, the projections will be wrong.

Suppose, for example, that employment of waiters and waitresses is projected to grow rapidly during the next ten years. Suppose also that this projection is partly based on the assumption that Americans will eat out more often during the next decade. Should the frequency of eating out instead decline, the demand for waiters and waitresses could be well below the projected level.

Another problem with much occupational information is that it does not give you all the facts you should have before deciding whether or not to enter a field. Many career information materials lack facts of particular interest or importance to women. They may not mention the number or proportion of women within an occupation, for example, tell whether women have risen to the top of the field, discuss the availability of part-time work, or tell how easy or difficult it is for women to reenter a field after taking several years out.

Much occupational information also ignores the many psychological and sociological aspects of work; it may not indicate the nonmonetary rewards—or the drudgeries—of an occupation, for example. Information about how a field may influence your own self-image, the image other people have of you, or your life-style may also be missing.

Despite all these limitations, you can still learn a great deal from published occupational information, particularly if you critically evaluate the materials you consult by taking the following steps.

1. Check publication dates and rely chiefly on the most up-to-date occupational information you can find.

2. Find out who published materials you consult, and ask yourself whether these publishers might have any vested interest in presenting biased pictures. Be especially wary of materials that paint a rosy picture of a field but make no mention of its bad points.

3. Check for completeness of information. Try to get all the facts outlined earlier in this chapter.

4. Use employment projections as a rough guide to future job prospects, not as a sure prophecy. Remember that even the best estimates of future employment opportunities within a field can easily go astray during the test of time.

5. Look for concrete, solid facts. It is not enough for occupational literature to say that pay in a given field is "good"; one person's notion of good pay may be another's idea of starvation wages. You need figures showing entry-level earnings as well as earnings of experienced workers.

6. Look for materials that describe occupational conditions within your city or state or in the geographic area in which you may prefer to work. Such materials should have information about local salaries, working conditions, and job opportunities. These facts will be more useful than the generalized descriptions found in materials prepared for nationwide use.

Sources of Information

The place to start looking for published occupational information is at your school counselor's office or your school's vocational counseling center. Counselors generally maintain a library of books, counseling magazines, leaflets, and other career information. Here, too, is where you are likely to find any occupational films, slides, or computerized counseling systems available at your school.

Many of the publications available in counseling offices list sources of additional information. Should you want still further details, consult your local public library. Many libraries have collections of career information published by government agencies, commercial publishers, associations of workers or employers in various occupations, and others.

A comprehensive guide to published career materials, including those which are free or inexpensive, is *Occupational Literature: An Annotated Bibliography,* written by Gertrude Forrester and published by the H. W. Wilson Publishing Company of New York City. This massive book catalogs career information materials by both title and occupation. It also lists publishers of career information and gives price and ordering information.

A growing amount of career information is now being published especially for girls and women. Foremost among publishers of information stressing this approach is the Women's Bureau within the U.S. Department of Labor. This agency publishes a wide variety of free and low-cost materials.

Among Women's Bureau publications that may be useful to girls investigating occupations are *Careers for Women in the 1970's, Job Training Suggestions for Women and Girls,* and leaflets describing opportunities for women in conservation, engineering, math, medical technology, optometry, personnel work, pharmacy, public relations, technical writing, and urban planning.

You can get a complete list of Women's Bureau publications with prices and ordering information by writing to the Women's Bureau, Employment Standards Administration, U.S. Department of Labor, Washington, D.C. 20210.

Several private publishers also put out occupational information especially for women. One is Catalyst, a national nonprofit organization attempting to expand job opportunities for college-educated women. Some Catalyst publications describe opportunities in specific fields—banking, communications, data processing, environmental work, fund raising, health services, and retailing and fashion, for example—and others tell women how to evaluate their talents, interests, and work goals and how to plan careers. Order forms and lists of publications showing prices are available from Catalyst, 6 East 82nd Street, New York, New York 10028.

Magazines are another source of career information directed to girls and women. For example, *Mademoiselle* magazine has a regular career feature that describes the nature of the work, earnings, and opportunities for women in specific occupations. Reprints of these articles are available, currently for 35 cents each. For a list of reprints and prices, write to *Mademoiselle,* Box 3389, Grand Central Station, New York, New York 10017. *Glamour, Seventeen,* and *Ms.* magazines also carry frequent articles about women in specific occupations, as does *The National Business Woman,* a magazine published by the National Federation of Business and Professional Women's Clubs, Inc. All these magazines are frequently available in public libraries.

Some associations of women working in specific fields also publish occupational information. Examples of such groups are the American Medical Women's Association and the Society of Women in Engineering. Names and addresses of these and other such groups are listed in association directories, which are usually carried by the reference departments of public libraries.

The National Federation of Business and Professional Women's Clubs, Inc. sponsors two career clubs—Nike for high school girls and Samothrace for college women—which also offer occupational information. Membership in either includes a subscription to a newsletter that contains articles describing opportunities for women in various career fields. For more information about these clubs, write to the National Federation of Business and Professional Women's Clubs, Inc., Program Department, 2012 Massachusetts Avenue, N.W., Washington, D.C. 20036.

One way to supplement the information you get from published materials is by talking with employers or personnel workers in agencies that hire workers trained in occupations that interest you. These people can tell you about educational and training requirements, job prospects, pay, advancement opportunities, and the nature of the work done in their firms. Unlike the generalities usually contained in published materials, these facts will be highly specific. In fact, they may apply only to the employer you consult. You should therefore ask whether the same facts are likely to hold for other employers in the field.

You may have a chance to talk with employers during career days or similar school counseling events. You can also call an employer's personnel department directly, explain who you are and what you want to know, and ask if you may set up an appointment with an appropriate company representative.

Employers sometimes conduct tours on which you may see workers in action. They may also permit you to visit work sites with a company representative. Such visits may give you only a glimpse of the work being done, but they will help to make occupations you explore more "real" to you. You will see for yourself where workers in the field are employed and their age, sex, and general appearance. You will watch them perform some tasks, and you may be able to tell whether the work surroundings are generally tense or relaxed, how fast or slow the work pace is, and whether workers look as if they are enjoying their jobs.

Talking to workers—particularly women—employed in fields you investigate is another way to learn about occupations. Such talks provide a good chance to get information not covered in published materials. For example, you can ask how an occupation influences a worker's life-style, what types of satisfactions it provides, whether the worker thinks it a useful and important field,

Girls exploring occupations should try to visit work sites to see the physical surroundings, get some feel for the pace of work, and learn what types of people are employed in the job. The work setting above is a factory in which plastic products are manufactured.

and what disadvantages the work holds. Workers should also be able to tell you how the pay and status associated with the occupation compare with those of other fields.

Persons employed in fields you explore may be able to give you an insider's viewpoint about the current state of the occupation and the changes that are likely to occur in the years ahead. Try to find out, for example, whether educational and job-training requirements are changing and how technology is apt to influence the field in the future.

Learn as much as you can about the opportunities for and experiences of women in the fields you explore. When you talk to a working woman, ask whether she has experienced any difficulty in finding jobs, getting choice work assignments, or receiving promotions. Check on the availability of part-time work and the ease with which women might combine work and family responsibilities.

If you can arrange it, try to spend a day or two on the job with workers you consult. Provided his or her employer does not mind, try your hand at work tasks you are capable of doing. This will help you get a better "feel" for the occupation.

Like published occupation information, employers' and workers' reports about their fields have certain drawbacks. Chief among these is that people you talk to will give you their own views and opinions based on their own experiences and biases. The views and experiences of others in the field will be somewhat different, and your own will be different, too, if you enter the occupation. You will not get "pure truth" from anyone you talk with, so do not accept any information as gospel.

Tryout work experiences are another way of learning about occupations. If you think you might be interested in becoming a newspaper or magazine reporter, for example, try to find a summer or part-time job with a newspaper or magazine. Even if you are not actually writing, you will be in a position to observe and talk to workers in the field and to learn a great deal about the conditions under which reporters work.

Some high schools have special programs that enable you to

work part time while attending school. Primarily in the business and sales fields, these programs, which will be described in detail in a later chapter, give you a good opportunity to learn about certain occupations.

Ultimately, however, the way you learn most about any occupation is by working in it full time. People who do not plan their careers carefully often use work experience as a trial-and-error method for finding a satisfying field. But drifting from one field to another, particularly when changes mean getting additional education or training, can be expensive and time consuming. It is easier—and far less nerve-racking—to explore the work world thoroughly before you start to work.

References

Darcy, Robert L. and Phillip E. Powell, *Manpower and Economic Education,* Love Publishing Company, Denver, 1973.

Isaacson, Lee E., *Career Information in Counseling and Teaching,* Allyn and Bacon, Inc., Boston, 1971.

National Vocational Guidance Association, *Guidelines for the Preparation and Evaluation of Career Information Media,* Washington, D.C., 1972.

U.S. Office of Education, *Career Education: A Model for Implementation,* 1971.

CHAPTER IV

Where Women Work

The number of jobs within our economy is enormous. The U.S. Labor Department's *Dictionary of Occupational Titles* lists more than 21,000 distinct occupations and 35,000 job titles. Of course, the number of occupations that will actually suit your interests, goals, and talents will be considerably lower than this. Many girls unnecessarily limit the number of fields they explore, however, and may thereby forfeit work that could bring a lifetime of satisfaction, by considering only occupations traditionally tagged "OK for women."

Most Americans associate certain occupations with men and certain others with women. The following riddle is based on this set of mind:

A father and his son were in an automobile accident. The father was killed immediately, and the son was rushed to the hospital for emergency treatment from a world-famous surgeon. After taking one look at the patient, the surgeon cried, "I can't operate on this boy. He's my son!" Question: How could the patient be the surgeon's son if the boy's father was killed in the accident? Answer: The surgeon was a woman, the boy's mother.

We tend to assume that surgeons are men, just as we tend to think that carpenters, bus drivers, welders, architects, police officers, and engineers are men. On the other hand, we expect secretaries, nurses, and home economists to be women and are surprised to hear of men in these fields.

Occupational titles themselves indicate that some fields are made up of women workers while others are staffed by men; repair*man,* mail*man,* steward*ess,* drafts*man,* and seamstr*ess* are everyday examples. (Federal government agencies and some other organizations recently changed some occupational titles to eliminate indications of sex, but the older forms remain in widespread use.

Occupational Fields and Workers

Girls planning careers need not and should not consider only occupations now associated with women! Before seeing exactly why, take a look at the fields in which most women do work.

The U.S. Bureau of the Census collects statistics showing both individual occupations and occupational categories in which workers are employed. Statistics for 1970 show that seven out of every twenty working women hold clerical jobs. About four out of twenty hold service jobs—relatively low-skilled jobs involving the preparation and serving of food, health care, hairdressing and other personal services, baby-sitting, and housekeeping work in homes and institutions, for example.

Slightly more than three out of twenty working women hold professional and technical jobs, those which generally require a college education, and slightly fewer than three out of twenty are factory workers. About one and one-half women of the twenty are sales workers, and less than one holds an administrative or management job. Women employed as skilled crafts workers, laborers, farm workers, and transportation equipment operators together add up to fewer than one out of twenty.

This breakdown contrasts sharply with the statistics for men.

More than four out of every twenty employed men are skilled crafts workers—carpenters, plumbers, electricians, mechanics, and printing press operators, for example. Very few women are in any of these occupations. Nearly three out of twenty hold professional and technical jobs, and about the same number are

COURTESY *Manpower* MAGAZINE

Although mathematics has gained a reputation as a "man's field," many women enjoy and succeed in scientific, engineering, and teaching occupations for which math is central.

factory workers. (These figures are similar to those for working women.)

More than two out of twenty male workers, far more than the number of women, are managers and administrators, and fewer than two out of twenty are in service occupations, the second-largest field for women. Slightly more than one out of twenty are in each of these areas: sales worker, laborer, and clerical worker. The remainder are farm workers and transportation equipment operators.

Because more women work in clerical jobs than in any other occupational category, it is not surprising that the single occupa-

COURTESY G. RICARDO CAMPBELL

The single occupation employing the largest number of women is that of secretary. Other popular clerical jobs include those of bookkeeper, typist, cashier, telephone operator, file clerk, and receptionist.

tion employing the largest number of women is that of secretary. Over 2,500,000 women worked as secretaries in 1970. The next most popular clerical jobs, in descending order of size, are bookkeeper, typist, cashier, telephone operator, file clerk, receptionist, keypunch operator, bank teller, statistical clerk, counter clerk, and stenographer.

Of women who work in service occupations, the second-largest occupational category for women, the greatest number—nearly 2,000,000 in 1970—hold food-service jobs, primarily those of waitress, cook, and food-counter and fountain worker. Over 1,-000,000 women service workers worked in the health field in 1970, usually as nursing aides, orderlies, hospital attendants, practical nurses, and health aides. Over 1,000,000 other women were private household workers (maids and housekeepers, for example).

Many women are employed in occupations that provide personal services, too. The largest occupation for women within this category is beautician. This occupation is followed in size by child-care workers and housekeepers who work in places other than private homes. The personal-service job of flight attendant, one that many girls consider very glamorous, employs only about one twenty-fifth of the women in personal-service jobs.

Most women holding professional and technical jobs are elementary- and secondary-school teachers. In fact, more than two fifths of all employed, college-educated women work as such teachers. Nurse is the second-largest professional job for women, followed, in decreasing order of employment, by accountant, college and university teacher, social worker, pre-kindergarten and kindergarten teacher, librarian, personnel and labor-relations worker, medical-laboratory technologist and technician, editor and reporter, physical or occupational therapist, and vocational and educational counselor.

Women employed in factories are most likely to be sewers and stitchers in clothing factories, assembly-line workers, or inspectors. Among women in sales jobs, the overwhelming majority work as salesclerks, and the second-highest number are hucksters and peddlers, women who sell items on the street or door-to-door. The third-largest sales occupation for women is that of real estate agent and broker.

A striking fact about nearly all the occupations that employ the largest numbers of women is that they are dominated by women. For example, over 90 percent of all secretaries, kindergarten teachers, child-care workers, registered nurses, practical nurses, private household workers, receptionists, telephone operators, typists, sewers and stitchers, stenographers, and beauticians are women. Women make up between 80 and 90 percent of all librarians, file clerks, bookkeepers, elementary-school teachers, cashiers, bank tellers, waitresses, and keypunch operators.

By contrast, the proportion of women in many of the occupations that employ the largest numbers of men is very low. For example, in 1970, women made up only about 2 percent of all engineers, yet engineering is the field employing the largest number of professional men. Women accounted for about the same proportion of mechanics and repairers, the largest craft occupation for men.

Why Women Work in Certain Fields

Why have women gravitated to certain occupations and virtually ignored others? A large part of the answer lies in society's notions about the kinds of work women can and should do. These are summed up in the familiar phrase, "Woman's place is in the home."

By and large, the occupations in which most women work today are extensions of the jobs they have traditionally done at home: caring for the sick, teaching children, weaving textiles, sewing, cleaning, writing letters, and preparing, serving, and preserving food. Following the industrial revolution of the 1800's, these jobs moved out of the home and into factories, large institutions, and offices. Women, who had done these jobs at home, were hired to do them in the work world. "Women's" occupations grew fast enough to absorb most of the growing number of women who chose to join the work force during this century, and female workers became concentrated in a limited number of home-related fields.

The status quo, the way things are, then came to be used as a justification for the way things should be. As more women entered so-called women's occupations, the myth grew strong that these were the jobs for which women are best suited. To this day, many people believe that women, as a whole, make good secretaries, nurses, and teachers, but lack the talent for fixing machines, driving, making financial decisions, setting business policies, or working with mathematical formulas or scientific theories. Women, many people assume, have the talent to become good typists but are incapable of making typewriter repairs; they are supposedly good at answering telephones but unable to improve their design.

Employers sold on the idea of "masculine" and "feminine" talents have not hired women for nontraditional fields. Often, they have not promoted women to supervisory or administrative positions even in fields they dominate because of the notion that management is a task for men. It is telling that in 1970, women elementary- and secondary-school *teachers* outnumbered men by more than two to one, but that nearly three times as many men as women were *administrators* in elementary and secondary schools.

Many women have also been convinced that there are "masculine" and "feminine" talents and have stayed away from "men's" arenas. Often, girls who excel in science or math or who enjoy such activities as driving or tinkering with electric appliances do not even think of pursuing a "masculine" occupation in these areas. Yet, there is no factual basis for believing that the aptitudes of men and women differ in ways that justify today's occupational patterns. Indeed, there are reasons to believe exactly the opposite.

Results of vocational aptitude tests widely administered to teenagers of both sexes show that many boys and girls share similar talents. For example, a combination of finger-hand dexterity, eye-hand coordination, and aptitude for space and form perception have been found almost as frequently among female as among male eleventh graders. However, relatively few women have entered some of the "masculine" jobs requiring precisely this set of abilities. These include such skilled trades as radio and television repairer, automobile mechanic, and business machine repairer.

Supporting the theory that men have not cornered the market on certain abilities is the fact that some women—in relatively small numbers to be sure—have been outstanding successes in nontraditional fields. Two famous contemporary examples of women in the male-dominated fields of politics and government are Golda Meir and Indira Gandhi. Mary Wells Lawrence, head of her own highly successful advertising agency, has been renowned in the business world. A woman scientist was head of the Atomic Energy Commission during the early 1970's, and a woman economist has served on the high-powered Council of Economic Advisers.

Less visible but far more numerous are the women who have entered and done well in such nontraditional fields as engineering, truck driving, medicine, law, and police work. Growing numbers of women are enrolling in apprenticeship programs, too, and working as plumbers, printing press operators, operating engineers (operators of heavy construction equipment), sheet metal workers, jet engine mechanics, and other kinds of skilled crafts workers.

Moreover, during times of manpower shortages, women have admirably performed jobs they are generally assumed unable to handle. "Rosie the Riveter" was a symbol for the many women who took over heavy industrial jobs during World War II. These jobs were formerly thought to lie outside women's abilities.

Not all women have the talent for nontraditional fields, of

course, just as not all men have the aptitude to become bankers or plumbers. But girls exploring careers need not dismiss any field simply because it has the reputation of being a man's domain. Men and women are individuals, each with his or her own unique blend of talents, interests, and limitations. These may or may not conform to common stereotypes, which tend to lump all men into one category, put all women into another, and neglect the individual differences that abound in both groups. For example, although men, on the average, are physically stronger than women, some women are stronger than some men. This destroys the supposition that women, as a group, are not qualified for jobs that require workers to lift or carry heavy items. Yet, women have been barred from some such jobs on the grounds that they are not strong enough to perform the work.

The notion of "masculine" and "feminine" talents is not the only reason women have become concentrated in certain jobs. Many women have been unwilling to undertake the long periods of preparation required by many professional occupations. This is one reason relatively few women are lawyers, doctors, and scientists. Women's tendency to stay away from such fields has probably been reinforced by books, television shows, and movies that portray women in such fields as lonely, unhappy women who are so serious about their work they have no time to enjoy themselves. These same women are often shown as unattractive spinsters. These stereotypes do not take into account the real-life women who have combined scientific or scholarly pursuits with marriage and children. Nor do they indicate that a woman who is seriously interested and absorbed in her own profession is apt to enjoy herself and to come into contact with a good many men with whom she can share both professional and personal interests.

Moreover, women have also failed to get the education or training needed to enter many occupations dominated by men. More girls than boys graduate from high school each year, but more men than women go on to post-high-school education and training. The tendency for women to forego skill training probably stems from the persisting myths that women work only for a few years before having babies, that they do not really need to prepare for employment, and that women cannot find real satisfactions in work anyway. No matter what their reasons for bypassing training, however, the consequences are clear: Women have wound up in fields with relatively low educational requirements. Many service and factory jobs are open to people with less than a high-school education. High-school graduates qualify for most clerical jobs. Girls who become practical nurses or beauticians need only a year or less of specialized training and need not be high-school graduates. Professional and technical occupations in which women dominate—librarian, nurse, elementary- and secondary-school teacher, and dietitian, for example—generally require only four or five years of college, less time than it takes to train for many other professional fields.

Another reason women have stayed away from nontraditional fields is that they have developed misconceptions about the kind of work these jobs involve. Many girls, for example, think engineers do strenuous, dirty, outdoor work. Actually, the majority of engineers hold sit-down jobs in modern offices and research laboratories. Another common misconception is that craft jobs require great physical strength. Yet many craft occupations—carpenter and electrician, for instance—offer work that is active but that requires no more strength than is needed to lift and carry a toddler and a bag of groceries at the same time.

Discrimination has also helped to determine where women work. Some employers have refused to hire applicants for certain jobs simply because they were women. Some training programs have been closed to women, too. These have included apprenticeship programs, high-school vocational courses in machine shop and woodworking, professional schools, and employer-sponsored training programs designed to prepare workers—*male* workers— for management positions. Although some such discrimination still exists, it is now against the law. Women may not be barred from employment or training programs solely on the basis of their sex unless the ability to do a job actually depends on a worker's sex.

Girls who neglect to explore certain fields because of stereotyped notions of "men's" and "women's" work, unwillingness to invest in training, misconceptions about nontraditional fields, or lack of knowledge about discrimination laws could be unnecessarily shutting out occupations that may suit their interests and talents better than occupations women have traditionally entered. That is the best reason for letting your own tastes determine the fields you explore.

Another reason not to ignore nontraditional fields is money. Inasmuch as this is the primary economic reward for working, it makes sense to look for adequate pay as well as personal satisfaction in work. But women workers are today at the bottom of the earnings heap.

In 1972, according to the U.S. Bureau of the Census, women who worked full time year-round earned a median income of $5,903. This means that half of all women who worked full time earned more than this amount, and half earned less. The median income for men, meanwhile, was $10,202—a whopping more than $4,000 more!

Part of this difference stems from the fact that women often gain less seniority and thus earn lower salaries than men because they interrupt their work lives for children. Part, too, comes from pay and promotions practices that discriminate against women. But the biggest reason for the earnings gap is that the fields is which most women work pay less than the fields most men enter. Women who worked full time in clerical occupations, the largest field for women, had a median income of $6,054 in 1972. This was considerably lower than the median of $10,413 enjoyed by men employed in craft occupations, the field that employs the largest number of men.

Many service occupations that employ the biggest numbers of women—private household worker, nursing aide, orderly, hospital attendant, waitress, and food-counter and fountain worker, for example—pay rock-bottom wages. Women who worked full time as private household workers had a median income of only $2,295 in 1972, and the median for women in other service occupations was only $4,483.

Women who worked full time in sales occupations earned even less than those in service jobs outside private households; their median was $4,445. By contrast, the median for men in sales occupations was $11,610. This enormous gap occurs because of the different kinds of sales jobs that men and women hold. Women in sales occupations are most likely to be salesclerks, hucksters, or peddlers. None of these offers good pay. Wages of salesclerks tend to hover around the hourly minimum set by federal law, and hucksters and peddlers often earn next to nothing. Men, on the other hand, are far more likely than women to be in sales jobs with high earnings potential. More men than women sell stocks and bonds, business machines, insurance, real estate, industrial equipment, and other high-priced items. Workers who sell such goods generally are paid commissions totaling a specific proportion—say 6 percent— of the dollar amount of their sales. Effective commissioned sales workers can thus earn very high incomes.

The highest-paid women are in professional and technical occupations. The median for professional women who worked full time in 1972 was $8,744, better than for all other women, but considerably lower than the $13,542 median for men in professional and technical jobs.

As in other occupational categories, the pay gap between professional men and women can largely be traced to the fact that occupations dominated by women pay less than others requiring a comparable amount of education or training. Consider teaching, the profession employing the largest number of women. The National Education Association reports that beginning elementary- and secondary-school teachers with a bachelor's degree earned an average of $7,357 during the 1972–73 school year, considerably lower than average starting salaries in many other professions. A survey by the College Placement Council showed that men who earned bachelor's degrees in engineering during the 1972–73 school year were offered starting salaries ranging from an average of $10,632 for industrial engineers to $11,448 for chemical engineers. Other average starting offers for men that year were $10,632 for accounting majors, $8,940 for men who had majored in business, and $10,368 for those who had specialized in computer sciences.

Smaller paychecks are not the only disadvantage of some of the jobs women have traditionally held. Some "women's" occupations —private household worker, waitress, factory worker, and nursing aide, for example—offer very few chances for advancement, variety, or the development of a worker's individual skills or talents. Workers in these occupations seldom have the freedom to exercise their own judgment, but must follow specific orders and repeat routine tasks again and again.

Similar limitations are built into some professional and technical jobs in which many women work. The nurse follows the doctor's orders with little opportunity to use her own judgment concerning patient treatment and care. Relatively few teachers can move up to supervisory or management jobs where they might help set school policies or make major administrative decisions. Physical and occupational therapists offer treatment only as prescribed by physicians. Social workers in welfare agencies may not be permitted to deviate from established policies, even when they think exceptions are in order.

Better Employment Fields for the Future

Girls looking for jobs that will help them develop their capacities for creativity, responsibility, and professional growth should be careful to see whether fields they explore offer opportunities to meet these needs. In some cases, nontraditional fields offer more of these kinds of challenges and satisfactions.

A further reason to explore occupations that fit in with your interests and needs but lie off the beaten path is that many will offer very good job prospects during the next several years. This is an especially important consideration for college-bound girls, inasmuch as the professional occupations women have traditionally entered are not expected to be able to absorb the growing number of women who will graduate from college in the next several years.

This situation has arisen mainly because teaching, a field that has for many years employed great numbers of female college graduates, is now a field in which job applicants outnumber jobs. The teacher surplus is expected to continue for some time, even though some types of teaching jobs—those in rural areas and inner city slums, for example, and those in specialties such as special and early-childhood education—are expected to offer good job prospects. Other professions that women have traditionally entered are not expected to offer enough employment opportunities to absorb all future female college graduates. Girls who want to maximize their chances of finding good professional job opportunities when they finish college should therefore look into some of the male-dominated professions where employment is expected to grow rapidly or where trained workers are expected to be in short supply during the next several years. A few such occupations are accountant, engineer, physician, chemist, bank officer, hotel manager, and business manager.

Employment prospects in many clerical and service occupations employing large numbers of women are generally expected to be good in coming years, but girls who do not plan to go to college may nevertheless want to consider other fields in which job prospects are expected to be equally good or better. Pay and advancement opportunities in these fields may be greater than those in "feminine" fields, and the nature of the work may better suit an individual girl's interests. Following are a few such occupations which girls do not ordinarily consider. These jobs generally require some specialized training beyond high school but do not demand a college degree.

1. Science and engineering technician. Workers in this broad and fast-growing occupational category help scientists and engineers do experiments, conduct laboratory tests, control the quality of manufactured products, solve specific scientific or engineering problems, and design or produce new products. The work generally calls for an aptitude for math, interest in working with scientific theories or mathematical formulas, and the ability to put theoretical knowledge to practical use. Only about 12 percent of the science and engineering technicians at work in 1972 were women.

2. Drafter. Girls who might enjoy making detailed drawings of buildings, bridges, and smaller engineered objects such as space capsules, typewriters, or television sets should look into drafting. Future job prospects in this field will probably be best for workers who complete drafting courses offered by technical institutes and

community and junior colleges, but job applicants who do well in high-school drafting courses are also likely to be in demand. In 1972, women made up less than eight out of every one hundred workers in the field.

3. Building trades worker. Among the fastest-growing building trades occupations are carpenter, construction electrician, plumber, and pipe fitter. Girls who like working with their hands, enjoy being outdoors, and prefer active to sedentary jobs may find these occupations very satisfying. Minimum union wage rates for building trades workers in large cities averaged more than $7 an hour in 1972. Training authorities generally recommend that building trades workers learn their skills through apprenticeship programs, but on-the-job and vocational school training are also available.

4. Appliance servicer. Workers in this occupation may fix appliances as small as toasters and irons or as large as refrigerators and washing machines. Demand for workers trained to fix electrical appliances is expected to grow fast in the coming years. Training for the field is available through high-school vocational courses, in federal job-training programs, and on the job.

5. Automobile mechanic. Girls with manual dexterity, physical strength, and an interest in cars and the way they work might consider the job of automobile mechanic. Job prospects in this field are now very good and will probably get better in the future. Skilled mechanics employed in large cities earned an average of more than $6 an hour in 1972.

6. Business machine servicer. The rapidly growing business machine industry will provide many thousands of job openings for service workers during the next few years. Opportunities for workers who can service computers and other data-processing equipment are likely to be particularly favorable. This field offers employment that is cleaner and lighter than work in most other

mechanical trades. Applicants for most jobs generally need a high-school education and may have to pass tests indicating mechanical aptitude, manual dexterity, or other aptitudes. In 1972 experienced servicemen—very few women are now in this occupation—earned from $150 to $250 a week.

All told, there are many good reasons to explore nontraditional fields when investigating occupations. To choose a nontraditional field simply because it is off the beaten path, however, makes as little sense as entering "feminine" occupations simply because tradition so dictates. The key factor in occupational choice, as in all facets of career planning, should be your own evaluation of the kind of work that will be most satisfying to you.

References

College Placement Council, *Men's Salary Survey: A Study of 1972–73 Beginning Offers by Business and Industry,* Bethlehem, Pennsylvania, March 1973.

Hedges, Janice N., "Women Workers and Manpower Demands in the 1970's," *Monthly Labor Review,* U.S. Department of Labor, Bureau of Labor Statistics, June 1970.

U.S. Department of Commerce, Bureau of the Census, "Consumer Income," *Current Population Reports,* Series P-60, 1973.

U.S. Department of Commerce, Bureau of the Census, *Occupation by Industry,* 1972.

U.S. Department of Commerce, Bureau of the Census, *We the American Women,* 1973.

U.S. Department of Labor, Bureau of Labor Statistics, *Occupational Outlook Handbook, 1974–75 Edition,* 1974.

U.S. Department of Labor, Women's Bureau, "Fact Sheet on the Earnings Gap," 1971.

CHAPTER V

Preparing for Work

"Be prepared." That slogan is best known as the Scout motto, but all girls scouting for future job satisfactions could adopt it equally well. Being prepared is the key to qualifying for jobs in the field you choose, and preparing for work means mastering job skills.

Types of Job Skills

Job skills are a combination of know-how and competence; they involve both knowing how to do particular tasks and actually being able to do them. You will probably gain the know-how needed in your field through study or instructions from others, but you will need to practice tasks on your own in order to gain competence. For example, a police cadet may learn how to direct traffic at an intersection from a lecture by a seasoned officer but will acquire competence in this job skill only after standing-in-the-street practice.

It is hard to overestimate the importance of good job skills. Skills are the human resources that employing organizations need in order to get their work done, the resources they seek and are willing to pay for. Throughout your work life, skills will be your most important asset for getting and holding jobs, for moving up, and for increasing your earnings.

Besides offering these economic benefits, skills can boost your feelings of worth and self-confidence by enabling you to feel competent and knowledgeable. They can also help to relieve the anxiety and tension most people feel when applying or interviewing for jobs; rather than feel that you are *asking* for work, your confidence in your own skills will enable you to feel that you are *offering* an employer important skills *in exchange for* fair payment.

Good job skills can also enhance your enjoyment of work. You tend to enjoy activities at which you excel more than those in which you feel inept.

You will probably need to gain two kinds of job skills as you prepare for the work world: 1. skills that are needed in nearly every occupation, and 2. skills that are unique to your chosen field.

Skills that are valued in a wide variety of jobs can be called *general* skills. Among these, one of the most valuable is the ability to communicate effectively through writing, speech, or both.

Nearly all workers must be able to understand written or spoken instructions and to express their own ideas clearly. Think of the minute-by-minute communicating required of teachers, office managers, waitresses, sales personnel, psychologists, company managers and supervisors, and all workers who deal directly with customers or clients.

Most industries need workers who can write or speak about products, services, or new ideas. They also look for people who can write technical reports, contracts, speeches, funding proposals, instruction sheets, training manuals, newsletters, program guidelines, and materials designed to build favorable public images. Employers also need workers who can give clear instructions to new employees, speak before client groups or other audiences, and explain management or personnel decisions to the workers they affect. In short, communications skills are assets to every worker who must work with others in the course of his or her duties.

Mathematical skills are also needed in nearly every field. The importance of these varies widely from occupation to occupation, but every worker needs to master at least the basics of counting, addition, subtraction, multiplication, and division. You will probably use these skills at least occasionally no matter what your job, and you will certainly need them to make sure your paycheck is accurate or to compute your new salary after you get a raise.

Salespeople, cashiers, waitresses, people who work behind counters in appliance-repair shops or other places offering customer services, bank tellers, and other workers who accept money from customers are among the workers who need to be able to add, subtract, and make change quickly and accurately. Numbers are the primary tool of accountants, stockbrokers, tax consultants, bookkeepers, auditors, mathematicians, statistical clerks, budget analysts, and managers who estimate business costs or keep track of profits. Scientists, engineers, and laboratory technicians often work with complex mathematical formulas, and social scientists —psychologists, economists, and sociologists, for example—and their research assistants all need a good knowledge of statistical methods. Architects and drafters make mathematical calculations, as do interior decorators, carpenters, and urban planners. In short, the list of occupations using mathematical skills is very long.

Organizing skills—reflected in the ability to structure people or things into units that work well—are also important in nearly every occupation and industry. Putting ideas and information into logical sequence is a big part of effective communications. Using time efficiently, arranging work space to best advantage, collecting the information and tools needed to do a particular job, and arranging files of correspondence or other materials so that they are easy to find and use are other examples of tasks requiring organizing skills.

Although organizing ability is important to all workers, it is often essential to administrative assistants and women who want to advance to jobs as office or business managers, factory fore-women, school or hospital administrators, coordinators of pro-grams or projects within an organization, or other workers with supervisory, administrative, or management responsibilities. Workers are often chosen for such jobs specifically because of their organizing skills.

Social skills and expertise in working cooperatively with others are further assets in most fields. You will need social skills in order to work on team or group projects, obtain information or assist-ance from other workers, get along with your boss, teach, super-vise other workers, or deal effectively with clients or customers. Doing any of these well often means developing such qualities as tact, patience, good humor, and sensitivity to others' needs and feelings.

A fifth general skill is the ability to make good decisions. This includes being able to define work-related problems or goals clearly, to gather and analyze information about possible solutions or strategies, and to anticipate both the good and bad conse-quences of different courses of action. The decision maker must then choose the alternative likely to work best in the given situa-tion.

On the job, you will almost certainly need to make some deci-sions about your own work. You may, for example, need to decide which of a number of assignments to do first or how to tackle a specific task or project. Many workers need to make decisions that will affect other people or their work as well. Professional health-care workers, police officers, supervisors, personnel workers, teachers, and guidance counselors are a few of the workers who may make such decisions daily.

Acquiring Skills

Where can you learn the general job skills just described? School is an excellent place to start. Most students are required to take prescribed courses emphasizing communications and mathematics, and other school activities can help you to develop the other basic job skills.

High schools offer a·variety of English courses, some of general usefulness, some intended for students going on to college, and others designed for those going into office work. Occupational literature and school guidance counselors can help you select the courses recommended for the field you have chosen. If you have not yet selected an occupation, take courses that are as advanced as your ability allows. No matter what field you eventually choose, you will probably benefit from practice in reading, writing, grammar, and speech.

In all communications courses, work at mastering these specific skills: reading quickly and with good comprehension; using good grammar and a vocabulary that expresses your thoughts precisely; and presenting your ideas clearly, concisely, and in logical sequence while writing or speaking. These are the basics of good communications.

You can get extra practice and gain proficiency in reading, writing, and speaking effectively through such extracurricular activities as debate, student government, and work on a school newspaper or club newsletter.

Most high schools offer a wide selection of courses that will help you develop mathematical skills. These include basic arithmetic, business math, algebra, geometry, trigonometry, statistics, calculus, accounting, and bookkeeping. Occupational literature and guidance counselors can help you select courses that will give you the best mathematical background for your field. If you must make such choices before you have settled on an occupation, it is best to take as many of the college-preparatory mathematic courses—algebra and geometry, for example—as you can master. Should you later decide on a professional or technical career, you will probably need these courses to get into college or other training programs.

And do not be frightened away from mathematics courses by the stereotype that math is "a man's field." As we have already seen, neither men nor women have exclusive claim on particular talents; many girls and women enjoy and excel at working with numbers.

High-school courses generally do not teach social, organizing, or decision-making skills as such, but opportunities to learn these skills exist in nearly every phase of school activity. Writing well-organized papers, making oral class reports, working on group class projects, deciding which homework assignment to attack first or how to do a science project, working cooperatively with teachers and classmates—all can help you develop skills that will eventually be useful on the job.

Extracurricular activities also offer opportunities to learn general job skills. Running a fund-raising event for a school club, coordinating production of a yearbook, chairing a student government committee, and planning a school dance all offer chances to build organizing, social, and decision-making abilities. It is often worthwhile to take part in such activities with the express goal of building skills like these.

Colleges, vocational schools, and other post-high-school training institutions offer advanced communications and math courses that can help you further develop these basic skills and relate them to your field. Many colleges and business schools also offer courses in business management, philosophy, logic, or personal-life management that may help students develop decision-making skills. On the whole, however, you will probably learn far more about making decisions, organizing, and getting along with people from life experience than you will from formal instruction. These general job skills are tools everyone needs for effective daily living as well as for job success.

Try noticing how often you need to make decisions, cooperate with others, and efficiently organize your time or activities in day-to-day life. Then consider the many opportunities you have to develop and improve skills in these areas. Just think, for example, how much practice you will get in making decisions as you plan your own career. If you feel you need help in developing any general life skills, do not hesitate to seek help from a school counselor.

Along with the basic job skills, most workers need *specific* skills that enable them to do the work of their particular occupation. Gaining specific skills usually includes obtaining an understanding of the facts and theories that underlie work in the occupation, learning how to use the tools of the trade, and mastering specific tasks and procedures.

For example, the primary work of medical technologists is making laboratory tests used in examining and treating doctors' and hospital patients. To perform their jobs, they must know certain facts about chemistry, biology, and mathematics. They must also understand the scientific principles upon which laboratory work is based and know how to use microscopes and other laboratory equipment. In addition, medical technologists need to be able to type and crossmatch blood samples, examine samples of body fluids and tissues under the microscope to detect chemicals or microorganisms, make cultures to determine whether bacteria or parasites are present in body fluids, and do other laboratory procedures.

Workers can sometimes learn specific skills without having a good grasp of the broad principles or theories underlying them. A medical technologist, for example, might learn how to perform a specific chemical test without knowing exactly how or why the test works. For several reasons, though, it pays to learn as much as you can about the "how's" and "why's" of your field.

One big advantage is that workers who know the principles behind their tasks generally do better work than those who do not. The carpenter who understands why different nails need to be used for specific building jobs is apt to turn out sturdier structures than someone who tries to remember which nail is used for which task without knowing why. If you work from memory rather than from understanding, you are more likely to make mistakes.

Knowing the principles behind your work makes it easier to resolve difficulties or problems, too. If a machine breaks down, knowing how that machine operates will help you to figure out what is wrong.

Most important, theoretical knowledge will help you to learn new job skills. Instead of trying to learn skills that may appear unrelated to knowledge you already have, you will be able to see how the new facts and procedures that you must learn are similar or related to other aspects of work in your field. You can then plug the new ideas into your old framework of knowledge.

It is in your best interests to be able to learn new skills with relative ease, for you are apt to need to master new competencies throughout your work life. Ours is a fast-changing economy, in which many jobs are frequently altered by new technological advancements, scientific discoveries, and theories. To keep up with such changes, workers in many fields need to be able to absorb new facts, master new procedures, and learn to operate or use new machinery or equipment. Being able to keep up with these changes and keep pace with changing job skill requirements will enhance your chances of finding job satisfaction and success.

You will probably need to learn some new skills every time you change jobs, too, and you will certainly need to learn new capabilities in order to move up. A promotion is generally both a reward for having already learned some skills and a challenge to learn new ones.

A solid grasp of the principles underlying work in your field will help you in all these situations. It will also offer a good jumping-off point for learning new skills in occupations related to yours. This will become important if you develop new work interests or think you would be more satisfied in another field, or if job opportunities in your occupation decline.

Where to Acquire Skills

Various avenues are open for learning specific job skills. The major ones are high school, junior and community college, vocational school, apprenticeship, college, employer training, the armed forces, and correspondence school. Each of these offers preparation for specific fields and job levels, and each has its own advantages and limitations.

High school. High-school graduation has become the standard for American workers. The majority of jobs are closed to workers who do not have at least a high-school education, and a diploma is a "must" for many types of advanced job training. More than three out of four young workers now hold at least a high-school diploma, and the proportion of students who finish high school is steadily rising. Girls who want to be in the running for promising jobs therefore need to get at least a high-school education.

For many students, high school is a prelude to additional education or training rather than an avenue for learning specific job skills. The majority of high schools do, however, offer training that prepares students for entry-level jobs immediately upon graduation.

Occupations for which high-school training is widely available include automobile mechanic, beautician, bookkeeper, carpenter, dental assistant, drafter, commercial-vehicle driver, farm worker, file clerk, food-service jobs, hospital aide or attendant, jeweler or watchmaker, practical nurse, salesperson, secretary, typist, welder, and various kinds of technicians, including those in design, electrical, electronics, and medical and dental laboratory work.

One big advantage of high-school vocational training is that it is free. Another is that it prepares students for entry-level jobs immediately after graduation. Girls from low-income families, and those who recognize the importance of job skills but who are unable or unwilling to get post-high-school education or training may therefore find high-school vocational training especially useful.

In addition, some—but not all—of the occupations offered in high schools will provide plentiful job opportunities in the years ahead. Good employment prospects are forecast for technicians, clerical workers, practical nurses, automobile mechanics, building trades workers, and drafters.

But high-school skill training also has its limitations. For example, some of the occupations for which training is offered are small, overcrowded, or becoming obsolete. They thus may provide relatively few job opportunities. Girls who intend to work immediately after high school should accordingly make sure they examine future job prospects in occupations for which they train.

Moreover, the entry-level jobs open to many graduates of high-school job-training courses often pay low wages, or require tasks many people consider routine, repetitive, or downright unpleasant. Even worse, workers may be unable to advance to better-paying, more interesting, or more responsible jobs unless they get additional education or training. Girls who take high-school training courses are therefore wise to consider the possibility that they may need to acquire further training either on or off the job in order to move up.

Often, too, the job skills learned in vocational high-school courses are too specific or too short on background knowledge to be easily transferred to related fields. Girls who want to change occupations may need to start "from scratch" in training programs completely unrelated to their former work.

Another difficulty is that employers in many fields for which high-schools offer training increasingly prefer workers with one or two years of training beyond high school over those with only a high-school diploma. The latest edition of the *Occupational Outlook Handbook* shows growing demand for secretaries, drafters, and many types of technicians with post-high-school training.

Junior and community college. Public and private two-year colleges offer one- and two-year programs that include both training in job skills and instruction in such academic subjects as English, math, history, and science. They prepare graduates for immediate employment and also provide education that can be transferred to four-year college programs. Graduates are awarded associate degrees or certificates indicating successful completion of vocational courses.

Fields for which junior and community colleges offer training include top-level secretarial work, nursing, and police work, plus a wide variety of occupations often called the "paraprofessions." These are occupations in which workers, who are generally called "technicians," "aides," "assistants," or "associates," support and assist professional workers by doing tasks that demand technical expertise but relatively little theoretical knowledge. Paraprofessional jobs for which two-year colleges provide training include library technician, forestry aide, dental assistant, dental hygienist, electrocardiographic technician, medical laboratory worker, occupational therapy aide, optometric assistant, physical therapy aide, X-ray technologist, surgical technician, engineering and science technician, drafter, food-processing technician, social work aide, teacher aide, counselor aide, and mental health technician.

Most jobs open to junior and community college graduates call for higher skill levels and pay higher salaries than those requiring only a high-school education. Moreover, junior and community college graduates generally enjoy plentiful job opportunities.

Public community and junior colleges can be a godsend for girls with relatively little money for job training. Tuition at these schools is generally low, and students can usually live at home and commute to classes, thus incurring lower living expenses than students who must pay for room and board while attending colleges or vocational schools away from their homes. As an added benefit, junior and community colleges typically offer both day and night classes, so girls who want or need to earn money while attending school can arrange work and class schedules to suit their own needs.

Two-year colleges are also a boon for girls who are not sure whether they want professional or paraprofessional status in fields that interest them. By going to two-year schools, they can get skill training that will prepare them for immediate employment in a paraprofessional job at the same time that they take the academic subjects required of college freshmen and sophomores. Girls who decide to opt for professional rather than paraprofessional jobs—

those who want to become, say, librarians rather than library technicians—can generally transfer junior college academic credits to four-year schools. The number of credits that four-year colleges will accept, however, varies widely according to the schools involved and their curriculum and course requirements. Girls who want to switch from a two-year to a four-year college should find out in advance about the potential for credit transfer by checking with admissions officials at both two- and four-year schools under consideration.

Girls considering community and junior colleges should also be aware that advancement opportunities for some two-year college graduates are somewhat limited. For example, paraprofessional workers may be able to take on progressively more responsible duties, but only up to a point. They generally cannot make independent judgments and decisions, counsel clients directly, or tackle some of the most challenging and complicated activities within their fields. These kinds of jobs are reserved for workers with full professional training. Paraprofessionals may, however, advance to positions where they supervise other paraprofessionals.

Vocational school. Business and trade schools and technical institutes provide short-term, intensive training for a wide variety of occupations. These schools, most of which are privately owned, profit-making enterprises, strongly emphasize vocational skills and offer few or no courses in academic subjects like English or history. The length of training at vocational schools usually varies from a few weeks to about two years, depending on the school and the occupation.

The largest number of private vocational schools are business and secretarial schools. Most of these teach office skills such as shorthand, typing, executive secretarial skills, comptometer or keypunch machine operation, bookkeeping, speedwriting, and court reporting.

Beauty culture and barber schools are also numerous, as are institutes offering training in fields such as practical nursing, drafting, commercial art, automobile repair, interior design, photography, fashion art, real estate, tax preparation, radio and television broadcasting, insurance, millinery, hotel and motel management, airline hostessing, modeling, and computer programming. Private vocational schools also train engineering and science technicians, electronics technicians, medical and dental laboratory workers, and paralegal workers.

Some nursing schools can also be considered vocational schools, even though they offer longer-term, more professional training than do other vocational schools. Nursing schools, which must be approved by state boards of nursing, generally have three-year programs combining classroom instruction with intensive clinical experience in hospitals and other health facilities. Students who complete nursing school study must pass state examinations to become registered nurses.

Vocational schools generally appeal mostly to individuals who are interested in learning specific job skills but who have no interest in or aptitude for academic subjects. Because they often offer day, evening, part-time, and full-time programs, students have the opportunity to learn job skills without enrolling in school full time and to combine training with paid employment.

Moreover, graduates of many vocational schools can expect plentiful job opportunities, both because of high demand for workers in some occupations emphasized in these schools and because some such schools—Katherine Gibbs Schools, for example, which teach secretarial skills—enjoy good reputations among employers. Many vocational schools enhance their graduates' chances of finding jobs by offering good job-placement assistance.

Not all vocational-school graduates, however, face good employment opportunities after graduation. Many, in fact, experience just the opposite. People who attend vocational schools that offer inferior or outdated training or preparation for fields that are already overcrowded may have a hard time finding jobs after training. Schools whose matchbook-cover ads or television commercials shout "Top Pay!" "Exciting Job Futures!" or "Make Money!" are often the very ones whose training is sadly deficient. Some states have enacted regulations covering standards of instruction and advertising statements made by specific kinds of vocational schools, but girls considering this avenue to job training need to ask local employers or offices of the Better Business Bureau about the reputation and past performance of any training school before they enroll. A free guide prepared by the Federal Trade Commission offers additional advice for choosing and evaluating vocational schools. You can get the *Pocket Guide to Choosing a Vocational School* by writing to the Federal Trade Commission, Consumer Information, Pueblo, Colorado 81009.

Students who enroll in private vocational schools must pay course fees that may be modest or relatively high, depending on the type of training offered, the amount of equipment needed for practice work, and the school's profit goals. Yet, training for many of the skills taught is available free or very inexpensively through public high schools and two-year colleges and adult education classes offered by local school systems. Moreover, paying for private vocational-school training in fields like keypunch operation and computer programming may be downright silly, because many employers give formal or on-the-job training to inexperienced beginners hired for these fields. Why invest time and money learning such skills at a private vocational school when you can earn money as you learn them on the job?

As with community and junior college training, vocational-school training is often of limited value to graduates who later want to move up on the job or transfer to related occupations.

Except for advancing to supervisory posts, for example, beauticians, typists, bookkeepers, practical nurses, and many technicians have little chance to advance to higher paying or more challenging positions without additional training.

Apprenticeship. Apprenticeship is a formal training system that prepares people to become highly skilled workers through a com-

COURTESY U.S. DEPARTMENT OF LABOR

Apprenticeship programs prepare both men and women for highly skilled craft jobs. Here, a printing trades worker who has completed an apprenticeship program prepares a magazine layout at a light table.

bination of on-the-job experience and related classroom instruction. Apprenticeship programs are available for some 350 different occupations, most of them blue-collar jobs calling for high-level craft, service, or maintenance skills. Examples are plumber and pipe fitter, electrician, carpenter, machinist, business machine repairer, automobile mechanic, meat cutter, jeweler, and printing press operator.

Apprenticeship programs often last four years, but may range from one to six years. Through this extensive training period, apprentices learn both specific skills and theoretical knowledge. For example, an apprentice construction electrician learns how to use, care for, and safely handle certain tools and materials; how to install electrical systems in homes, offices, and industrial settings; and how to repair and service wiring systems. The apprentice also gets classroom instruction in electrical layout, blueprint reading, math, and electrical theory.

Apprenticeship programs are generally conducted jointly by employers and labor unions. They are most common in heavily unionized occupations.

Apprenticeship has traditionally been a man's domain. In the past several years, however, the number of women apprentices has, with good reason, grown steadily. Increasing numbers of women are recognizing that apprenticeship programs offer practical, thorough training for many skilled jobs that pay very well. Moreover, apprentices earn while they learn. Apprenticeship agreements usually spell out starting rates of pay for new apprentices and provide for regular increases until the completion of training, when wages reach those of fully trained workers in the craft.

Another advantage of apprenticeship is that the combination of classroom instruction and on-the-job skill training gives workers a good background for learning related skills with relative ease. For example, a fully trained construction electrician can easily transfer to other types of electrical work.

Like their male colleagues, girls who want to go into apprenticeship programs generally need a high-school diploma or the equivalent and may need to meet age or other entrance requirements. Some female applicants may encounter resistance from sponsors of apprenticeship programs or from male apprentices who believe that women should not or cannot be apprentices. Unless there is a real reason why her sex prevents her from doing work in a craft occupation, however, it is against the law to discriminate against a woman in apprenticeship programs solely because she is a woman.

Further information about apprenticeship programs is available from the apprenticeship agency within your state government. Write to the State Apprenticeship Agency in care of your state capital for details. You can also learn more about apprenticeship from the nearest office of the Bureau of Apprenticeship and Training of the U.S. Department of Labor—addresses are shown in the white pages of the telephone directory under U.S. government listings—and from your nearest local public employment office, listed in the telephone directory under state government agencies. Unions and employers can supply details about apprenticeship programs in their fields.

College. Colleges and universities prepare students for professional and academic occupations. They offer all necessary training for the occupations of teacher, engineer, home economist, chemist, economist, psychologist, and historian, and provide preliminary education for physicians, dentists, and others who must attend post-college professional schools such as law or medical school. Colleges and universities are also among schools that offer training for nurses and other health professionals.

Most college students must elect a major field of study and take a relatively large proportion of courses that emphasize knowledge and skills central to this field. Most schools offer majors in fields that are clearly related to specific occupations—engineering, accounting, and elementary education, for example—as well as in broader subject areas such as chemistry, English literature, or zoology.

Some students minor in a second field. This means they take a substantial number of courses in this field, but not as many as in their major field. Students who choose both major and minor fields can delve into two areas that interest them and may widen their job options by learning skills in both.

No matter what their major or minor fields, college students usually must take general courses designed to give them at least a smattering of knowledge about a variety of subjects that colleges deem important to an all-around education. These may include such areas as English literature, composition, history, philosophy, foreign languages, and art or music appreciation. These fields are among those called the liberal arts, and they form the basis of a college liberal arts curriculum.

A liberal arts curriculum does not offer students skills or knowledge related to a specific occupational field. Instead, it aims to help students learn about the nature of human beings and their society, and to develop intellectual and communications skills. Liberal arts students may concentrate on one or two subject areas—American literature, English literature, philosophy, French, or fine arts, perhaps—or may choose a general arts and sciences program that offers a broad sampling of many liberal arts subjects.

It usually takes at least four years to get a college education, and some college programs in engineering and other fields take a minimum of five years to complete. At the end of this time, graduates are awarded a bachelor of sciences degree, or, in the case of liberal arts majors, a bachelor of arts degree.

Bachelor's degree holders can earn advanced degrees through additional graduate study; one or two more years of study are usually required for a master's degree, and at least three or four years of graduate study are needed to earn a Ph.D. (Doctor of Philosophy).

Workers in many professional fields increasingly need advanced degrees in order to qualify for top-level jobs. Social workers, psychologists, librarians, and urban planners, for example, generally need at least a master's degree to qualify for professional work in their fields. Engineers and business administration majors who get master's degrees boost their chances of finding good jobs with good pay, and some states require elementary and secondary teachers to earn master's degrees within a certain number of years after they begin teaching.

Mathematicians, college teachers, scientists, and social scientists who do top-level research or theoretical work are among workers who usually need a Ph.D. Doctors, lawyers, dentists, and veterinarians need to earn advanced professional degrees by completing professional-school study. Professional-school programs usually take at least three years; and physicians must put in a minimum of seven years of medical school and hospital training.

Despite the amount of time required, a college education can be the most profitable investment a girl might ever make. On the whole, professional occupations pay more than jobs requiring less education, and professional workers are far less likely than clerical, blue-collar, or technical workers to be unemployed. Professional jobs can pay off in job satisfaction, too, by offering challenging and interesting work. Professional workers generally enjoy pleasant working conditions and relatively high social status as well. These facts may help explain why surveys show that professional workers are more satisfied with their jobs than clerical and blue-collar workers, and why they are more likely to say they would choose the same occupations if they had to do it again.

But college is an expensive investment; besides requiring much time, commitment, and energy, a college education requires a large dollar outlay. A year's expenses for tuition, room and board, student fees, books, and personal needs at top-notch private colleges can easily mount up to $5,000 or so a year. Multiply this figure by at least four, add on allowances for future inflation and increases in college fees, and the cost can be phenomenal.

There are, of course, less expensive colleges, including many public schools whose fees are relatively modest. Moreover, girls set on professional careers may be able to cut down on costs by living at home and commuting to a local college. Student loans, part-time jobs, and scholarships are also available to strongly motivated girls with good academic ability.

"Motivation" and "academic ability" are key terms here, for these should be central factors behind any girl's decision to go to college. Girls who go to college simply because their parents can afford and expect it, because they don't know what else to do, or because "everybody from my neighborhood is going," are doing themselves an injustice by failing to look at their own interests, abilities, or goals, And do not accept blindly the assumption that you *need* a college education to get a good job. Only about 20 percent of the jobs that will open up during the next several years will require a four-year college education, according to the U.S. Department of Labor, even though many others will require some kind of training beyond high school.

Going to college to "find yourself" can also be a mistake, even though many girls do learn a great deal about themselves and their interests while in school. Unfortunately, however, many others drift through college and, upon graduation, are no closer to knowing what they want out of life than they were four expensive years earlier.

Girls who enter college without clear-cut career goals often choose a liberal arts curriculum in the hopes that a general, well-rounded education will help them discover work-related talents or interests. Because a liberal arts education does not emphasize occupational preparation, however, it is easy for liberal arts students to postpone career planning. Girls considering a liberal arts education should therefore be prepared to make a conscious effort to discover their career interests and aims. They should also be aware that a bachelor of arts degree does not open the door to

jobs as easily as college training that includes occupational preparation. Some employers tend to be wary about liberal arts graduates without immediately usable job skills because of the time and
money involved in training them for jobs. Others view liberal arts
graduates who are uncertain about their future plans as poor
employment risks. The theory here is that such graduates are
taking a trial-and-error approach to learning about the job world,
and that they are as likely as not to quit their jobs before their
productive efforts repay employer training costs.

A wide variety of fields is open to liberal arts graduates, however, usually those in which a well-rounded education, ability to
learn, and communications skills are more important than specific
job skills. Such fields include administrative work, computer programming, newspaper reporting, personnel work, sales, advertising, banking, book and magazine publishing, government, and
insurance. Many new liberal arts graduates vie for work in these
fields, however, so job competition is often keen. Moreover, liberal
arts graduates generally are paid lower salaries on their first jobs
than are graduates with occupational skills in such specific fields
as accounting or engineering.

Girls who enroll in liberal arts programs can enhance their
employability by developing career plans and goals as early as
possible. They might also take at least some courses that offer
occupational training. Courses in journalism, personnel administration, magazine editing or production, sales, and market research are among those that mesh well with a liberal arts education.

Keep in mind, too, that liberal arts majors can build employment skills outside the classroom. Relevant extracurricular activities and summer and part-time work experience may also boost
graduates' opportunities for putting bachelor of arts degrees to
work.

Workers in many occupations gain their skills from on-the-job training. Through informal instruction at the private employment agency where she works, this employment counselor has learned how to search out job openings, test and interview job seekers, and match applicants with available jobs.

Employer training. Many employers offer their own training for skills needed within their organizations. Such training takes on a variety of forms, but the most common is informal, on-the-job training in which workers are taught specific skills as the need for them arises. Such training is generally short on theoretical instruction, focusing instead on individual job skills.

Many occupations for which informal on-the-job training is available are relatively low-skilled (and often low-paying) occupations. They include waitress, cook, hospital attendant, building custodian, factory worker, cashier, salesclerk, duplicating machine operator, shipping and receiving clerk, bank teller, receptionist, doctor's office receptionist, and social work aide. On-the-job training is also available for some occupations requiring more technical skills. Examples are service and repair occupations such as automobile mechanic and appliance service worker. High-school graduates are generally preferred for all these jobs, although some employers will train applicants without a high-school diploma.

Many employers conduct more formal training programs for new employees. Lasting anywhere from a few days to several months, such programs may prepare workers to operate keypunch or tabulating equipment, run switchboards, write computer programs, service or repair business machines, sell real estate or stocks and bonds, sell manufacturers' products to retailers, or install and service telephones and switchboard equipment. Applicants for such training generally need at least a high-school diploma, and those with college degrees are often preferred for sales and computer programming training.

Many large companies and government agencies also conduct management training programs in which new employees work for a relatively short time—say several months—in one unit within an organization, and then move on to another division. This kind of rotation, which may last a year or two, is designed to help trainees develop a feeling for work procedures and management techniques throughout the organization. At the end of training, workers elect to join the office or unit that suits them best. Large banks often run similar training programs for bank officers. These programs are generally open only to college graduates, but experienced company employees who lack college training but show potential for management jobs may also be accepted.

Besides management training, which often includes short-term workshops and seminars as well as rotating assignments, many employers also provide other kinds of training for employees who want to learn more advanced skills. They may conduct classes through which file clerks learn to type, for example, or typists learn to take shorthand to qualify for higher-paying positions. To encourage their employees to get more schooling, some companies also pay all or part of the costs of work-related college courses or other educational programs in which employees enroll.

Like apprenticeships, employer-sponsored training programs have the advantage of allowing you to earn money while you gain skills. Moreover, the training offered by many organizations is solid, thorough training that enhances a worker's chances of earning promotions or of moving to other employers who offer higher pay or better working conditions.

On the other hand, some employer-sponsored training relates only to work done by that organization and therefore cannot be readily transferred to other employers. For example, companies that manufacture business machines may train workers to repair or service only machines made by that firm. Workers who want to move to a different employer may be unable to do so without additional training. Thus, workers with company training may be "stuck" with the employer that trains them. Workers trained on the job for relatively low-skilled positions may also be "stuck"— not necessarily with one employer but in occupations with low pay and few opportunities for advancement.

Correspondence school. Although employers generally do not recommend them as the best preparation for employment, correspondence courses do offer the opportunity to learn many vocational skills. Most home-study courses are prepared by private, profit-making organizations, but some are offered by state universities, the armed forces, and other public institutions. Correspondence course enrollees pay for books and lesson plans, which are sent to their homes. Students complete assignments and may need to return them to the school for evaluation. Course fees vary according to the type and length of training, the sponsor, and the quality and quantity of practice materials and services provided students.

Skills taught through correspondence courses include typing, bookkeeping, accounting, clothes design, drafting, photography, hotel management, and real estate sales.

Home-study courses also offer academic subjects at both the high-school and college level, so that girls who have dropped out of high school or who have financial or other difficulties that make it hard for them to attend college can take such courses at home.

Another advantage of correspondence study is that it may offer the chance to learn skills that are not taught locally. This can be particularly important to girls living in small towns and rural areas. In addition, correspondence courses allow students to set their own study schedules and progress at their own rate of speed.

Several big problems exist, however. One is that not all correspondence schools are competent or honest. Some make exaggerated claims or offer poor training. Some states have enacted laws regulating correspondence schools, but many others have not. Girls interested in correspondence schools therefore need to check carefully with local employers or training authorities about the merits of individual schools and programs. Another way of investigating correspondence schools is by consulting the "Directory of Accredited Private Home Study Courses" which is free from the National Home Study Council, 1601 18th Street, N.W., Washington, D.C. 20009. The directory lists schools approved by the council and tells how to learn more about schools that are not listed.

Some courses offered by correspondence schools on a fee basis are available free in local public high schools or quite inexpensively through community adult education programs. Girls considering home study should therefore check to see whether the training they want is available locally.

Correspondence courses are best suited for individuals who are highly motivated and who can work independently without the reinforcement and pressure that come from attending classes and having to complete assignments by a given time. Girls without these traits who start correspondence courses may never finish them.

The armed forces. The Army, Navy, Air Force, and Marine Corps all offer many training and educational opportunities for women. They train new recruits, who must generally have at least a high-school diploma or the equivalent, for a wide variety of jobs in fields from communications, medical services, clerical work, administration and management, public information, recruiting, machine and engine maintenance, fire fighting, and electronics, to supplies management. Training is available for both "desk" and "field" jobs, and the Navy trains women for jobs aboard seagoing ships. Armed forces training is geared to specific jobs within the services, but some skills—those in medical services, clerical work, administration and management, engine maintenance, and electronics, for example—are transferrable to civilian jobs.

The armed forces also pay college and nursing-school expenses for young women who agree to serve on active duty for a specified number of years after graduation. For example, coeds who participate in college ROTC (Reserve Officers Training Corps) programs can receive $100 a month (for up to ten months a year) during their junior and senior years. To receive these payments, they must agree to serve as armed forces commissioned officers for from two to six years after college. An ROTC cadet must spend about three hours a week studying military history and strategies, drilling, and learning field techniques and attend a six-week summer camp.

Servicewomen are eligible to take free and very inexpensive correspondence courses prepared by the U.S. Armed Forces Institute. These range from the elementary-school to the college level, and more than 1,200 colleges and universities accept credits earned through this program. In addition, the federal government helps pay tuition fees for servicewomen who study at accredited colleges while off duty. Many colleges offer convenient courses on military bases.

After their terms of enlistment, women are eligible for the same veterans' benefits awarded men. Among these are monthly educational payments made to veterans who enroll in college or vocational schools.

Women who sign up get relatively good pay, have opportunities to work throughout the country and at bases abroad, can travel by plane free or at reduced fares during the thirty days of paid vacation they get each year, and receive free—or get allowances for—food, clothing, and lodging. Armed forces members also receive free medical and dental care and can shop at commissaries—armed forces grocery stores—or in post exchanges resembling department stores. Prices in both are lower than in civilian stores.

Many girls find the opportunities and benefits of uniformed life very attractive. Those girls who object to following orders they may not agree with, obeying many rules, living on or near military bases, or being part of a rigid social system based on rank may be unwilling to pay the armed services price for training and education. And there is no chance to try on uniformed life and see how it fits. Once a woman signs up, she is obligated to serve for the full term of her enlistment, even if she later finds that she dislikes service life. Neither men nor women can resign from the armed forces as they might quit an unsatisfying civilian job.

Military recruiters and high-school counselors have details about armed forces training opportunities, educational benefits, and entrance requirements. Girls considering this avenue to job skills should find out in advance whether military skills that interest them can be transferred to civilian jobs.

The Necessity for Some Type of Training

Inasmuch as different kinds of education and training lead to different occupations, the type you will need to get depends primarily on the field or specialization you choose. Your personal preferences, long-range career goals, and ability to meet entrance requirements will also enter into your decision, particularly when there are several ways to prepare for your field or many schools to choose from.

Your financial resources may also affect your selection of a specific kind of training program or a particular school, but *lack of money is no excuse for foregoing training altogether.* As already noted, public high schools provide free vocational training, and public two-year colleges generally offer inexpensive courses. Apprenticeship programs and company-sponsored training enable you to make money while learning skills. Scholarships, loans, and work-study arrangements are available for college and private vocational school students. And the armed forces offer free training plus veterans' benefits that can finance college or other training after enlistment.

Like lack of money, the desire to get married is another unacceptable excuse for bypassing job training. Unfortunately, girls who believe the old notion that wife and mother are the most satisfying—if not the only—roles for women often neglect job training and marry before finishing high school, immediately afterwards, or before completing work for a college degree. Many give up their own career aspirations and work to support husbands enrolled in colleges or professional schools. Although marriage is, of course, important to most women, foregoing training in order to marry is a very shortsighted move. Remember those statistics showing the number of years women work outside the home and the number of marriages that fail? Moreover, a woman who earns only a "P.H.T." (Putting Hubby Through) degree is apt to find herself doing housework or working at a relatively low-paying, routine job while her husband gets the prestige, pay, and job challenges associated with professional work.

One way to combine marriage and job training is to postpone marriage until after you have finished the kind of training you want. If you do get married earlier, try to figure out how both you and your husband can learn occupational skills. You might both work part time and go to school part time, for example, or you might go to school full time while your husband supports you and then switch roles after you have completed training. Getting your training first may forestall any temptations to stretch a "temporary" interruption in training into a permanent one.

Girls who become pregnant and subsequently drop out of high school or fail to enter other educational or training programs are also taking a very shortsighted view, especially because such mothers may already be or may one day become their child's sole support. Trying to raise a child on one unskilled worker's paycheck can be economically difficult and emotionally heartbreaking.

Women with children may need to surmount large obstacles in order to gain education or training. For example, mothers with low incomes or none at all may be unable to scrape up money for training, baby-sitting, or both.

Such problems are difficult—but not impossible—to solve. Social service agencies, low-cost day care centers, and job-training programs for the disadvantaged may provide some assistance.

Local public employment offices, listed in the white pages of the telephone directory under state government agencies, can provide counseling, details about local job-training programs, and other help.

How to Choose Job Training

No matter what occupation you want to prepare for, try to make sure you are investing your time and money in the highest-quality training you can get in view of your aims, aptitudes, and budget. Consider the alternatives carefully before you make a decision, and look for training programs that will prepare you for the kind of job, pay, and advancement opportunities you want. To get the facts you need in order to choose a training program wisely, you might take the steps below.

1. Ask school counselors, local employers, and public employment office counselors to recommend training or educational programs for the occupation you choose.

2. Write to business, trade, or professional associations in your chosen field for a list of accredited training programs or other information about schools or training programs. Names and addresses of such organizations are listed in career information sources such as the *Occupational Outlook Handbook* and in association directories available in reference sections of public libraries.

3. If you are considering a company-sponsored training program, talk to company employees or other employers in the same business to find out whether the training offered is thorough and up to date, leads to good job and promotion opportunities, and can be transferred to other companies.

4. Consult individual college catalogs and directories such as *Barron's Guide to the Two-Year Colleges, Barron's Profile of*

American Colleges, and *Lovejoy's College Guide* to learn about the size of a school's student body and faculty, the courses it offers, entrance requirements, and costs. These publications, often available in counselors' offices and school and public libraries, also indicate whether colleges are coeducational, for women only, state-supported, private, or affiliated with a religious denomination.

5. Visit schools offering training to examine facilities and surroundings and meet students and staff members. Look for well-equipped training rooms and laboratories, an extensive library, and experienced instructors with reputable credentials. When visiting a campus on which you may live, examine dormitories and dining facilities, and try to learn about campus life by talking with students already enrolled. These steps will help you assess the quality of the education or training offered and decide whether the school suits your personal tastes and preferences.

6. Girls who need extra money for college can get information about scholarships, loans, and work-study programs from school counselors, college catalogs, financial assistance directories found in many school and public libraries, college financial aid offices, local banks, and state departments of education. Write to the U.S. Office of Education, Division of Student Assistance, Bureau of Higher Education, Washington, D.C. 20202 for information about federal financial aid programs for college students.

Once You Have Chosen

Once enrolled in any kind of educational or training program, take it seriously. If you have a choice of courses, select those which emphasize useful information or skills over those which require little effort but also teach little. Remember that your basic aim is to prepare for adult life, not to "get by" with a minimum of work.

If you have a chance to become a student member of a trade or professional organization within your field, it may be well worth while to join. Such a membership may give you inside information about changing skill requirements, new specialties, or employment prospects within your field. This knowledge may enhance your ability to choose courses or a specialty that will increase your chances of getting a good job.

And do as well as you can in your training or course work. Some girls underplay their abilities and work at less than their potential because they think boys shun girls who are "too serious" or "too brainy." However, it is better to live up to your own abilities and to develop them to their fullest than to squeeze yourself into conventional notions of how competent or intelligent girls should be. Girls at the top of their classes can walk through job doors closed to others. A good school record may also help you convince employers that you are interested in and have the aptitude for the field you have chosen. This will be especially important in talking to prospective employers who believe the unfavorable stereotypes about women workers described in the next chapter.

Furthermore, many boys—mostly intelligent boys—*like* bright and capable girls. You will probably feel more comfortable with boys who like you because of your real abilities and talents than with those with whom you must "play dumb." How long would you want to be untrue to yourself and keep up that kind of pretense?

References

Arnold, Arnold, *Career Choices for the '70's: Realistic Ways to Select and Achieve Your Goals,* Macmillan, New York, 1971.

Stevenson, Gloria, "The Paraprofessions," *Occupational Outlook Quarterly,* U.S. Department of Labor, Bureau of Labor Statistics, Fall 1973.

Stevenson, Gloria, "Putting a Bachelor of Arts Degree to Work," *Occu-*

pational Outlook Quarterly, U.S. Department of Labor, Bureau of Labor Statistics, Winter 1971.

Stevenson, Gloria, "Women: Uncle Sam Wants You," *Occupational Outlook Quarterly,* U.S. Department of Labor, Bureau of Labor Statistics, Winter 1973.

U.S. Department of Labor, Bureau of Labor Statistics, "Job Prospects in the 1970's Outlined in New Guide" (press release), April 3, 1972.

U.S. Department of Labor, Bureau of Labor Statistics, *Occupational Outlook Handbook, 1974-75 Edition,* 1974.

U.S. Department of Labor, Women's Bureau, *Training Opportunities for Women and Girls,* 1960.

CHAPTER VI

Finding a Job

No matter what occupation you select and prepare for, at times during your work life you will need to be a salesperson, someone who knows how to "sell" her talents, skills, ideas, or personality traits to others. You will also need to be a smart consumer, shopping for the "best buys" in the job market. To land your first full-time job, you will probably have to combine both roles, selling your talents to the employer offering the most promising job you can find.

Many girls are terrified of job hunting and dread the prospect of approaching employers and applying for work. Apprehensions are perfectly understandable, for job hunting can be a very trying process. In a way, job applicants put themselves on the line; they say to employers, "Here I am. Here are my qualifications. Do you want me?" Whenever employers say "No, thanks," job seekers have to be able to take the situation in stride, bounce back, and apply for other jobs without suffering needless feelings of personal rejection or worthlessness. In addition, job seekers usually must take the initiative in finding leads, contacting employers, and applying for work. This active attitude may be difficult to sustain during a long stretch of job hunting.

Job hunting can be hard work for both men and women, but female job applicants often face an added difficulty: they may have to battle employers' reluctance to hire women. A fact of life is that many employers hold unfavorable views about women workers. Among these are opinions that women's place is in the home or only in certain jobs; that women do not take work seriously and

COURTESY U.S. DEPARTMENT OF LABOR

One way to overcome job-hunting jitters is by having the skills that qualify you for the kind of job you want. Here, a woman is learning the laboratory skills required of pharmacists.

work only for "pin money"; that they are "too emotional" for the business world; that they miss more work because of sickness than men do; and that they are poor employment risks because they are apt to quit work to marry, have babies, or move to a new location if their husbands are transferred.

All these views can be disputed. How, for example, can women's place be in the home when more than half of all working-age women are employed? How can women's place be only in a few occupations when experience and results of aptitude tests indicate that women can master a very wide range of tasks and skills? As for women working only for "pin money," statistics show that nearly half of all women who work do so because of pressing economic need; they are either single, widowed, divorced, or separated, or their husbands earn less than it takes to support a family adequately.

Studies have also shown that there is little difference in men's and women's work absentee rates because of illness or injury. One study by the Public Health Service shows that women, on the average, miss 5.9 days a year for health reasons, compared with 5.2 for men. And although it is true that many women do leave work for marriage and children, an employer has no more guarantee that any given male employee will not quit to take another job than that any given woman will quit for family reasons.

As for women workers being "too emotional," exactly what does that mean? The business world appears to tolerate the behavior of male executives who explode with anger after a business setback or when things go awry, yet such reactions are quite "emotional." Besides, any categorical statement about the emotions of all women fails to take into account the many differences in individual reactions to given circumstances.

You could raise all these points with employers reluctant to hire women, but you would probably have little chance of changing employers' minds through argument. First, many employers do not openly express their hesitations about women workers. It is therefore impossible to dispute them. Moreover, people's attitudes do not change easily. As the old saying goes, "My mind is made up; don't confuse me with facts." Because of the human tendency to resist another's attempts to persuade one to change, you may best fight employer stereotypes about women by letting your actions and manner indicate that you are a person who is seriously interested in work, who knows what she wants in and from a job, who is acquainted with the demands of the work world, and who has gained the skills needed to work in her chosen field. Take a thorough and realistic approach to job hunting.

Preparation for the Hunt

Assuming you have already chosen an occupation and prepared for it, try to figure out which of the many variations of work within that occupation might suit you best before you launch your job search. Perhaps you will be able to narrow your employment goals down to a specific kind of job—perhaps, to sell life insurance or be a private secretary to a business executive. If not, choose several job alternatives for which you are qualified. You might look for work as an editorial assistant, editorial researcher, copywriter, or reporter, for example.

Clarify any preferences you have about working in a specific geographic location or for a particular type of employer—a large organization, small office, government agency, profit-making concern, or whatever. Decide, too, how much money you want to earn and what types of advancement opportunities are important. Try to form at least a tentative idea of the kind of income and work you would like to enjoy after working for five years.

To avoid unnecessary disappointment, be realistic about your job goals. Find out local pay rates for the kind of entry-level work you are seeking, and expect offers you get to be comparable. Expect, too, to start close to the bottom. Beginning jobs in nearly all fields offer more routine assignments, less opportunity to work independently, and less opportunity to be creative or to be in control of work processes than do jobs open to workers with several years' experience.

You can also avoid undue disappointment by being somewhat flexible in your job goals, especially if you are looking for work in fields or geographic areas where jobs are scarce or competition keen. The same holds true if you are job hunting when unemployment rates are high or economic conditions slow. Under these circumstances, prepare yourself for the possibility that you may need to settle for working conditions, pay, or job duties that fall short of your aims in order to achieve your overriding goal of finding a job that comes as close as possible to meeting your needs and wants. Do not settle for so little, however, that you will be unhappy on the job. Determine instead where and how much you can compromise and still expect to be satisfied.

In fields where you expect tough job competition, you might hold alternative job plans in reserve. Suppose, for example, that you want an editorial job on a fashion magazine. Such jobs (as your exploration of occupations should have indicated) are hard to find, and if, after much looking, you cannot locate one, you might alter your goals somewhat. For example, you might elect to look for an editorial job on a trade journal or some other publication where you could gain editorial experience. A year or two of such experience may open the doors fashion magazines close to beginners. Or you might take some other kind of job in the fashion industry and use this as your entrance to writing about the field. Or you might decide to take a secretarial job on a fashion magazine in the hopes that you will later be promoted to an editorial position. Be careful if you choose the latter alternative, however, for although secretaries often are promoted to professional-level positions—particularly in fields like advertising, public relations, radio and television, book publishing, and magazine work—many employers who indicate that they offer such promotions rarely do. To assess realistically your chances of being promoted from the secretarial ranks in any organization, get specific facts about the number of such promotions made recently; or try to speak to someone who knows the employer's policies, someone working in the firm's secretarial ranks, or someone who has been promoted from them.

Having clear—but flexible—job goals in mind should give you a sense of purpose and direction that will help overcome job-hunting jitters. Approaching employers and taking the initiative may be somewhat easier because you recognize that you are seeking something that you want. Knowing clearly what you are looking for also spotlights the "shopping" aspects of job hunting. Realizing that you are assessing employers and their jobs every bit as much as they are evaluating you should give you an extra measure of confidence.

You can raise your confidence level even further by knowing precisely what skills, abilities, and personal strengths qualify you for the kind of job you want. If you have the appropriate education and training needed for your field, you should be able to look back over your preparation and see what skills and knowledge that you possess qualify you for the kind of job you want. With these firmly in mind, you should know exactly what assets you have to offer an employer. Pinpoint specific achievements or honors that will show employers you can do the work. Did any school projects indicate outstanding skills or abilities? Do good grades indicate aptitudes or skills needed in the kind of work you are seeking? Have you won any prizes that show others' recognition of your abilities?

Also review your extracurricular activities, part-time and summer job experiences, hobbies, and volunteer work for other evidence of your ability and for signs that you possess the personality traits needed in your field. If you are looking for a job that requires organizational or social skills, for example, or the ability to convince others of your point of view, think back to experiences that reflect such traits. Consider any special skills that may be useful on the job, too, such as ability to drive a car or knowing how to operate specific machines or equipment.

Preparing a Résumé

Besides helping you pinpoint job-related assets, this kind of inventory will give you the information you need to prepare a résumé, a concise, written statement showing the kind of work you want and your qualifications for doing it. Applicants for professional, technical, administrative, and managerial jobs generally need résumés. So may those seeking sales and clerical positions.

You can use your résumé in several ways: enclose it with a job-application letter; take it to an employment office when you apply in person for a job; take it or send it in advance to an employer when you go for an interview; and leave it on file at personnel offices in firms where you might like to work but which have no openings at the time you apply.

Keep your résumé brief and to the point. Busy employers want the pertinent facts about your background in as few words as possible, so try to limit your summary to one page. Résumés should be typed, and you will need a number of copies to distribute to prospective employers. These may be printed or photocopied, but do not use carbon copies because they tend to smudge and look messy.

There are several ways to organize your résumé, but the following format should be useful to most young women seeking their first full-time jobs: Begin with your name, address, and telephone number. List your employment goals next. If you are looking and qualified for several related jobs, list them in the order of your preference.

Show your education and training next. If you are a high-school graduate, indicate the school you attended, the date you graduated, any scholarships or honors you received, and extracurricular activities related to your job goal. Give similar facts about any colleges or vocational schools you have attended, and indicate the degrees or certificates you received, your major and minor subjects, and other pertinent course work. (You need not summarize your high-school education if you have attended post-secondary schools, but you may do so if your high-school course work, activities, or special projects reflect outstanding abilities or skills.)

Your work history should appear next in your résumé. List part-time, full-time, or summer jobs you have held, starting with the most recent and working back. Show the dates you were employed, the name and address of the employer, the nature of the employer's business, and the position you held. Then describe your duties briefly. You will find it easier to be brief and to the point if you start each sentence with a verb. For example, say "Operated switchboard," "Took dictation," or "Assembled electrical components." Emphasize the duties requiring most skill and judgment. If you worked with special types of equipment, specify them; for typing and shorthand, state the number of words per minute.

If you served in the armed forces, your résumé should show your branch, length of service, and rank, as well as the kind of training you received and the nature of your duties.

When appropriate to your job goals, your résumé should also contain such information as knowledge of foreign languages; pertinent volunteer or leisure activities; membership in employee or professional organizations; licenses or certifications to perform specific kinds of work; and any relevant articles you have published or other special achievements.

Also supply the name, address, telephone number, and position of two or three personal references—people who know you and can vouch for your character. Try to get references from people of good standing in the community—say a physician, rabbi or pastor, school principal, or prominent business person. Teachers and professors under whom you have studied are also good references. Make sure, however, that you get the permission of people you list as personal references before you use their names. Because your previous employers are already listed in the work experience section of your résumé, do not list them as personal references.

End your résumé with information about your marital status and other personal data. Many employers are very interested in knowing whether female job applicants are married or have children, and there is a reason for listing these facts *after* your qualifications. List them earlier and employers with a bias against hiring, say, unmarried women, or women with children may fail to read or consider seriously the rest of your résumé should you fall into these categories. Better to let employers know your marital situation after you have "sold" your job qualifications. You may, if you like, also indicate your birthdate and any geographic preferences for work. If appropriate, indicate whether you are willing or free to travel, and whether you have a driver's license and a car.

Two examples will show you ways in which to organize your résumé. Use these only as general guides, however, not as rigid outlines. Because your résumé is basically a selling tool, an advertisement for yourself, your overriding concern when setting it up should not be format but presenting your job assets in such a way that employers will recognize that you are well qualified for the kind of work you want.

RÉSUMÉ

Nancy R. Kent   (Date of résumé)
487 Franklin Drive
Woodland, N.Y. 10124
Telephone: (914) 422–8780

POSITION WANTED

Reporter, desk person

EDUCATION

New York University, B.S., cum laude, 1974.

Major: Journalism. Minor: Psychology. Other courses: beginning and advanced photography.

Extracurricular activities: Copy editor and reporter on college newspaper.

Honors: Sigma Delta Chi award for outstanding college reporting during the 1973–74 school year.

WORK EXPERIENCE

Summers of 1972 and 1973. Copygirl, *Woodland Gazette,* 456 Hunter Avenue, Woodland, N.Y. Covered city council meetings. Wrote obituaries. Wrote and took photographs for a feature series of a community arts group. (Attached is a one-sheet photostat of clippings of articles I wrote for the *Gazette.*)

Summers of 1970 and 1971. Public relations aide, Woodland YWCA, 765 Binter Street, Woodland, N.Y. Helped to write copy for leaflets advertising fall program of clubs and classes.

HOBBIES

Photography, cooking, travel.

SPECIAL SKILLS

Good reading, writing, and speaking knowledge of Spanish.

PERSONAL REFERENCES

Mrs. Mary Simms, President, Woodland Business and Professional Women's Club, 234 Sutter Street, Woodland, N.Y. (914) 512–6623.

John Sell, Ph.D., Professor of Journalism, 433 Beaux Arts Building, New York University, 485 West 65th St., New York, N.Y. 10003. (212) 771–2231.

PERSONAL DATA

Single, no dependents.
Born August 18, 1952.

(Date prepared)

RÉSUMÉ

Carole A. Anderson   Position wanted:
111 Second Avenue   ARCHITECTURAL TECHNICIAN
Williamsport, Pa. 17701
Telephone (418) 432–8801

EDUCATION:

Williamsport Area Community College, A.A.S. in architectural technology, 1974.

Williamsport Area Junior-Senior High School. Graduated third in a class of 340. Took college preparatory course with elective classes in mechanical drawing and drafting.

WORK EXPERIENCE:

Summers of 1972 and 1973. Tracer, Standard Engineering Products, Inc., 277 Timothy Street, Williamsport. Prepared drawings for reproduction by tracing them on plastic film.

Summer of 1971. Receptionist, Cole Brothers Insurance Co., 485 Wilton Street, Williamsport. Greeted visitors; answered phones; opened and routed incoming mail.

STUDENT ACTIVITIES:

Represented Williamsport Area Community College at the National Architectural Students' 1973 Conference on Environmental Quality, sponsored by the American Institute of Architects.

Published research paper prepared for cost estimating course in *Contractors' Monthly,* April 1973.

REFERENCES:

William Comers, Instructor of Graphic Arts, Williamsport Area Community College, Room 560, Washburn Building, Williamsport, Pa. 17701 (418) 773–2890.

Marilyn Hendricks, Principal, Williamsport Area Junior-Senior High School, Williamsport, Pa. 17701 (418) 452–8871.

PERSONAL DATA:

Single, no dependents.
Born March 8, 1954.
Prefer employment involving opportunity to visit construction sites. Have car and driver's license. Willing to relocate.

Finding Employers

Once you know what kind of job you want and have your qualifications clear in your own mind and on your résumé, you are ready to start the actual job hunt. The first step in this process is finding employers who are offering the kind of jobs you are looking for.

If you start looking for a full-time job while you are still enrolled in school, you probably have a direct pipeline to a variety of employers. Agencies with jobs to fill often send recruiters to high schools, colleges, and business and trade schools to interview graduating students. High-school guidance counselors and the counselors in post-high-school placement offices can tell you when such recruiters will be at your school, the types of jobs they have to fill, and the kind of educational background applicants need in order to qualify.

You will probably have to register with your school's placement office in order to be eligible to set up interviews through the school, so check on such requirements well before you start job hunting—say at the beginning of your last year or semester in school or midway through a short-term training program. Find out, too, how you can get up-to-date information about scheduled recruiter visits. Some schools post monthly schedules, hand out photocopied calendars showing scheduled visits, or list recruitment activities in school newspapers.

Not all employers recruit directly at schools, of course, so even if you use your school's placement services, you may need to come up with other job leads.

You should, for example, regularly look through the classified advertisements in newspapers and in professional journals or trade magazines in your field. Employers often use such means of advertising specific job openings. Newspaper want ads often contain more listings for clerical, service, and factory jobs than for professional openings, whereas professional journals emphasize occupations that require a college education, and trade magazines concentrate on jobs in their respective businesses and industries. Besides pointing to openings, want ads can give you insight into salaries and the number of opportunities available locally or in your field.

Employment agencies also know where many jobs are. Participating employers list their job openings with such agencies, and agency personnel counselors refer job seekers registered with the agency to these employers.

Employment agencies can be classified into two broad categories: those that charge fees for their services, and those that do not. State employment services, public agencies set up under a federal-state cooperative arrangement, offer free placement services. They also provide free counseling and career consultation and offer job seekers free aptitude tests and tests of proficiency in such job skills as typing or shorthand. More than 2,400 state employment service offices exist across the country, and their addresses are listed in the white pages of telephone directories under the state government listings. If you live in a small town or rural area that has no local office, your post office should have the address of the office nearest you. If you write there for information about local job vacancies, enclose a copy of your résumé.

State employment service offices in all major cities and many smaller ones maintain computerized lists of all openings within the local metropolitan area. This means you have to register at only one office in order to learn about vacancies registered with several offices in your locality.

Most jobs listed at public employment service offices require less than a college education, and many are for relatively low-skilled occupations. Many cities, however, have special offices for workers seeking professional and managerial jobs. These have lists of local vacancies as well as information about professional job openings in all parts of the country.

Unlike the state employment service, private employment agencies charge a fee for their job-placement services. In some cases, fees are paid by employers who list job openings, and applicants pay nothing. In other cases, however, applicants who get jobs through private agencies must pay the fees. These may range from about 4 percent to 10 percent of your annual starting salary, depending on the nature of the job and the geographic area. At the top of this range, such fees are substantial.

If you register with a private employment agency, you will probably need to sign a contract that shows your responsibilities for paying fees and their amount. Read this contract carefully, and make sure you are willing to pay the agency's price before you sign. You may be able to avoid paying fees altogether, however, if you are looking for work in an occupation where workers are in great local demand. You may be able to find this out by checking newspaper want ads; a large number of listings for workers in your occupation signals good demand. In this kind of situation, you may be able to register at an employment agency on the condition that you will consider only jobs for which employers pay agency fees. Should you take this approach, state your position clearly before you sign a contract, and be sure the terms of the contract are in accord with your stand.

Private employment agencies vary in quality. Some are first-rate, but some entice job seekers to register by running newspaper advertisements for jobs that do not exist, and some waste both employers' and job seekers' time by sending applicants to interview for jobs for which they are not qualified. Agencies that run newspaper want ads with long lists of jobs and those whose ads emphasize glamour jobs are often the worst offenders. To determine which are likely to be most reliable, talk to people who have used local private employment agencies. If you have any questions about a particular firm, inquire about it at your local office of the Better Business Bureau.

In the past several years, a small number of agencies that offer job counseling and referrals specifically for women have been set up across the country. Examples are Washington Opportunities for Women, located in Washington, D.C.; Women's Place, Inc., in Los Angeles; and Options for Women, in Philadelphia. Such agencies offer a variety of services, and they often charge fees. To find out whether any such agencies exist in your area and whether they may be of help, check with local groups interested in employment opportunities for women. These might include the local chapter of the National Organization for Women, the nearest office of the Women's Bureau of the U.S. Department of Labor, a local business and professional women's club, or your state commission on the status of women.

Some unions and professional associations also keep track of openings in their fields. If you belong to such an organization, it pays to see whether it maintains a register of openings or job-placement service.

Another way to find out about employers who are or may be hiring workers in your field is by asking friends, family members, teachers, neighbors, and other likely acquaintances. These people may know of vacancies in firms or agencies where they work or they may have heard of openings with other employers "through the grapevine."

If you learn about job openings through personal contacts, do not expect to be hired simply because you are "Muriel's friend," or "Herb Peterson's daughter." After all, you probably do want to be hired on your own merits—on the basis of what you know rather than who you know. On the other hand, do not hesitate to accept a person's offer to recommend you to an employer or to help you set up a job interview because you do not approve of using "pull." There is a great difference between relying on "pull" to get you a job for which you are not qualified and accepting help in finding work that you can do competently. And you need not feel obligated to accept a job that does not appeal to you simply because someone "was nice enough" or "went to all that trouble" to get you and an employer together. Your first obligation is to find a job that will satisfy you, and you are shortchanging yourself if you accept any job you do not really want.

Several sources of information are available to girls interested in government jobs. The personnel office of your city or county government can provide information about local openings, and your state civil service commission has information about openings in state government. These offices can tell you what jobs are available, which agencies are hiring, educational and training qualifications, pay, and application procedures. You may have to pass competitive examinations for some jobs or meet other specific requirements.

Check with the U.S. Civil Service Commission for information about federal job openings located in Washington, D.C., across the country, and overseas. The federal government is the biggest employer in the nation, and it offers jobs in a wide variety of occupational areas.

Federal jobs are filled on a merit basis; applicants must qualify on the basis of competitive examinations and ratings of experience and education. Civil Service examinations for entry-level jobs are given several times a year in cities across the country, and are administered at many high schools, colleges, and other schools. Local offices of the Civil Service Commission can supply information about openings and application procedures. Their addresses are listed in the white pages of telephone directories under the U.S. government listings. You may also write for information to the U.S. Civil Service Commission, Washington, D.C. 20415.

Besides using the sources already described to find information about actual job vacancies, you may also want to approach employers who hire workers in your field on the chance that they may be hiring. You can get names of employers who use people with your skills by checking under the appropriate classification in telephone directory yellow pages.

In addition, local chambers of commerce and boards of trade can often supply lists of local employers. You might also check business or industrial directories available at local libraries. (These generally do not circulate, so be prepared to copy down employer names and addresses while at the library.)

Another possible source of information about employers who might hire people in your field is the business section of newspapers. Articles about businesses that are expanding or setting up branch offices may indicate firms hiring additional employees.

And do not overlook the possibility that local telephone, electric, and gas companies may have job vacancies. Utilities companies hire people for a wide variety of fields, including areas such as telephone operating and secretarial work, in which many women have traditionally been employed.

Applying for Work

After learning of employers who have definite openings or those which may need people with your skills, you need to get in touch with these employers. Counselors at school placement offices and employment agencies often act as go-betweens, but in other circumstances you generally must contact employers on your own.

You can do this in one of two ways: by telephoning or by writing a letter of application. With local employers, it is easiest to telephone to explain who you are, what specific job or what kind of work you are looking for, and how you heard about the job opening or the firm. Call the person in charge of the company division or unit that has the opening, if you know who that is. Otherwise, telephone the personnel office, or, in small firms, the head of the company.

Letters of application are appropriate when you approach employers who live in other localities, and when you are answering a want ad that directs you to write to a given address. Although letters of application vary considerably, according to the kind of work you want and the circumstances, they should always tell which position or what kind of work you want and how you learned about the opening or the firm.

Enclose a résumé, but include in your letter a brief summary of your qualifications. This should be designed to catch the employer's interest. Your letter should also suggest an interview. For nearby firms, you may even indicate that you will phone to make arrangements for an interview within a week or two. Should you say you will call, however, make sure you do. Why risk antagonizing an employer by failing to do what you promise to do? Even if the employer has nothing suitable for you when you first apply, you may want to apply for future openings and good will can be important.

Letters of application should be brief, neat, and businesslike. Type them on plain 8½-by-11-inch business paper, and limit them to one page. Whenever possible, address them to specific company officials, too, because letters to designated individuals may get more prompt and careful attention than those addressed to a firm or a title such as "personnel director."

Following is a sample letter of application:

> 455 Gadsden Hall
> Drake University
> Des Moines, Iowa 50311
> (Date)

Mr. David P. Evans
Vice President for Sales
American Business Machine Company
200 Waterloo Street
Sioux City, Iowa 51106

Dear Mr. Evans:

An article in yesterday's *Sioux City News* reports that your company has broken ground for a new wing to accommodate expanding sales operations. I will receive my B.S. degree in business in June, and would appreciate being considered for a sales position should you be hiring at that time.

During my last two years at Drake University, I worked part time as a commissioned salesperson for the Arundel Office Furniture Company. My success in this position, plus my enjoyment of college sales courses, makes me think I could be effective and personally satisfied representing a firm like yours. I have also held several summer clerical jobs and think my understanding of the needs of secretaries and office managers will enhance my ability to "close."

A résumé of my qualifications is enclosed. I would appreciate a personal interview to discuss my application further and will call your secretary within a week to discuss a possible meeting.

Sincerely yours,

Roberta F. Dyson

The Interview

Preparing a résumé, getting names of prospective employers, and writing letters of application are all preliminary to making face-to-face contacts with employers in job interviews. Interviewing is the most critical—and can be the most anxiety-provoking —part of the job-hunting process. If you have gone through the steps previously described, however, you have already started to prepare for a successful interview by developing the confidence that comes from knowing what you want in a job and knowing what assets you have to offer an employer.

If you are job hunting through a school placement office or employment agency, counselors there will probably schedule interviews for you. In other cases, employers that you contact will suggest interviews and you will need to set a mutually convenient time.

Schedule interviews at least two hours apart, longer if you need more than half an hour to travel from one to the next. Giving yourself plenty of time eliminates the tension of feeling hurried and the chance that you will need to cut off one interview in order to go to another.

Dress neatly and appropriately for interviews. Workers tend to dress more casually today than they did in the past, but avoid wearing very casual clothes like blue jeans or slacks cut like jeans to your first meeting with an employer. On the other hand, do not overdress in party or evening clothes. A simple, businesslike dress or pants suit, high heels, and simple makeup or jewelry are most likely to be in order. If you are in doubt, play safe by erring on the conservative side.

Prepare in advance for interviews by finding out as much as you can about the employing agency. What products or services does it provide? Is it a local establishment or part of a regional or national network? What are its prospects for future growth and profits? Does it have a reputation for being either a good or an undesirable employer in its field?

You can get some of these facts from business or industrial directories. Many local public libraries maintain files of corporate annual reports, and these may also give you valuable information about a company. Check with friends or relatives who have had experience with or know about the employer. You might also stop by the agency's public-relations or personnel office a few days before your interview to ask for any in-house leaflets describing the agency. These publications may help you understand the kind of image the employer wants to project as well as offer concrete information about the firm and what it does. This kind of research will give you some basis for evaluating the employer in terms of your own interests and may suggest questions to ask during the interview. Focusing on the employer during this kind of preparation may also help you lose self-consciousness and feel more confident during the interview.

You also need to collect any materials you need to take with you before each interview. Take along at least one copy of your résumé, if you have one. Even if you have already sent a copy to the employer, you may need an extra or you may want to glance at it when answering questions about dates of employment or other details. Take your Social Security card, too, or your Social Security number. If you do not have one, apply for a card at the local district office of the Social Security Administration before you go to the interview. Addresses are in the white pages of the telephone directory under U.S. government listings.

If you have not supplied the employer with a résumé, be sure you have details about your education and experience at your fingertips, and take along the names and addresses—telephone numbers, too, for local people—of both business and personal references. You might also want to take along a pad and pencil to jot down any important information or remind yourself of employer requests for additional information.

Prepare, too, to be on time. Better yet, plan to arrive five or ten minutes early. Check and double-check the employer's address in advance, and make sure you know how to get there. If you are traveling by bus, check bus schedules and routes well ahead of time. If you drive, give yourself plenty of time to park. Some employers are rigorous about punctuality, and there is no sense in making a poor impression by being late for an interview.

Either before or after the interview, you may be asked to fill out the employing agency's application form. To make sure you do a neat and thorough job—remember employers are apt to form opinions about your work habits on the basis of the way you fill out application forms—take your time. Read over the entire form first, and make sure you understand the directions and questions. Note such details as whether you are to answer questions in blanks above or below the lines. Be accurate, especially about dates, your Social Security number, spelling, and punctuation. When you have finished, double-check to make sure you have not left any blanks or made mistakes.

Some employers require aptitude or skills tests as part of the application procedure, and these may be administered immedi-

ately before an interview. Try not to worry about your performance on such tests; instead, concentrate on answering the test
questions or doing the tasks you must do.

Listen carefully to instructions for taking tests, and be sure to
ask questions if you do not clearly understand what you are expected to do. Many tests have time limits, which will probably
be explained in advance. In these, work steadily and carefully, but
not frantically. Once you begin, do not light a cigarette or do
anything else that interrupts your work. Do not spend too much
time on any one question; skip difficult or time-consuming ones,
and come back to them when you have finished the others. And
after the test is over, try not to reproach yourself for not doing
better or to worry about the results. You can make better use of
your energy by concentrating on the interview itself.

Interviews are meetings between human beings with unique
personalities, and the most successful interviews are often those
in which each person relaxes and lets his or her "real self" come
through. "Successful interviews," incidentally, are here defined as
those in which interviewer and job applicant realistically learn
about each other and decide whether or not their interests mesh,
not as interviews that result in job offers.

As in all meetings between people, courtesy is appropriate at
job interviews. Consider the interviewer your "host" or "hostess,"
and wait for him or her to invite you to sit down and to guide
the interview. If you want to smoke, ask if the interviewer minds.

Friendliness and a sense of humor are also appropriate at job
interviews, but flirting is not. Although a male employer may
enjoy responding to a flirtatious job applicant, he is probably not
apt to make a hiring decision on that basis. He is, after all, in
business to make money and to get work done.

Be as attentive as possible at job interviews. Pay close attention
to the questions asked by the interviewer, and try to answer them
briefly and to the point. Rambling on and on may be a sign of

nervousness. If you catch yourself talking more than you usually do, try to relax.

Pay attention to the interviewer's manner, too. You may learn a great deal about the interviewer this way—including the fact that he or she is nervous, too. You may also be able to tell whether the interviewer is reacting positively or negatively to things you say or do.

Do not make the mistake, however, of trying to figure out what kind of person the interviewer wants and then trying to be that person. Besides being unfair to yourself and to an employer—after all, you want work that interests the "real" you, and the employer wants a worker who meets certain criteria—trying to meet expectations you think an interviewer holds is likely to make you feel so uncomfortable and insecure that you will not be able to show the best qualities you actually do possess.

Sometimes, interviewers will begin with a vague statement like, "Tell me about yourself." This is your cue to explain what kind of job interests you and why. The more specific you can be, the better. Avoid such broad statements as saying you are interested in personnel work because you "like people." So do lots of workers who hold other kinds of jobs.

Similarly, answer such questions as "What are your future job goals?" or "Why did you apply to this company?" as specifically as possible so that you give the interviewer a clear picture of your job interests and preferences.

When talking about your job qualifications, describe them frankly without either exaggerating or downplaying them. If the interviewer asks whether you have a skill you have not actually mastered, say so. If, however, you have learned related skills or if your past achievements indicate an aptitude to learn that skill, emphasize these facts if you are interested in the job.

The interviewer is likely to be interested in your marital status or plans, and it pays to be honest when discussing these. If you are engaged or pregnant and you are planning to work for only a short time, say so. Misrepresenting yourself may enable you to get a job with this employer this time, but it is likely to cut down on your chances of being rehired should you want to return in the future. Moreover, lying about your employment plans perpetrates employers' stereotypes about the undependability of women workers and makes it harder for other women to get jobs.

If you are already married or a mother, you may need to assure the employer that your family responsibilities will not interfere with your job. You may need to describe your child-care arrangements, for example, or say that your husband is not likely to be transferred to another location. You need not volunteer such information, however, but wait for the interviewer to inquire.

Although it is a general rule to let the interviewer guide the meeting, do not be afraid to ask questions, especially if the interviewer offers you a job or indicates that you are being seriously considered. This is the time to find out exactly what your duties would be.

This is the time to find out about opportunities for advancement with the company, too. The interviewer will probably give you some idea of the promotion possibilities that will be available, but knowing that many employers have been lax in promoting women, you may want to get specific facts about the company's record. This is particularly important if you are taking a secretarial job in the hope of being promoted to a professional slot. You may ask about the company's past record for promoting women directly—without being rude or belligerent, of course—or you can try to look around the agency and see for yourself how many women hold positions to which you hope to advance.

Many personnel specialists feel it is unwise to ask about salary, vacations, or employee benefits until you have a definite job offer on the theory that employers will assume you are more interested in the pay than in the work. However, some interviewers will ask, "What salary do you want?" Provided you have done your homework and have a realistic idea of average starting salaries in your occupation and locality, you can reply by stating your requirements. Or you might respond by asking what the company pays new employees in the position for which you are applying. Many employers have standard starting salaries and pay scales.

Incidentally, the salary figures used during job interviews (like those that appear in want ads) indicate "gross" earnings, the amount a worker makes before the employer withholds money for taxes, a retirement plan, and health insurance or other programs to which workers may contribute. Single workers with no children take home roughly between two-thirds and three-fourths of their gross income after all withholdings are made. Take this difference between gross pay and take-home pay into consideration when determining your income requirements and looking at starting salaries.

In the event that you are offered a job during the interview, do not accept too hastily. Unless you are absolutely certain that you want it, give yourself some time to think about the pro's and con's of the position (every job has both), and tell the interviewer you will call with your response by a certain day. In the interests of courtesy, be sure to follow through with this call, even if you decide not to accept the offer.

Employers who do not offer jobs immediately may clearly state that the firm is unable to use you or may indicate that they will get in touch with you within a certain time period to let you know the decision. If an employer does neither, ask when you may call to get a definite "yes" or "no." If you are asked to return for another interview, note the time, date, and place. Employers often interview job candidates two or three times before making a final selection and may have you talk with several people within the agency, such as a personnel representative, division director, and the person who would be your immediate supervisor.

Should an interviewer indicate that the firm is unable to hire you, you might ask for suggestions about other employers you may contact. And no matter what the outcome of the interview, thank the interviewer for his or her time.

It is generally unrealistic to expect your first interview or your first job application or your first employer contact to pay off in a job you enjoy. Remember this to avoid undue disappointment or discouragement. Try also to remember that it often takes time, patience, and persistence to find a job that feels "right" to you, but that the rewards of satisfying work are well worth the effort required to achieve them.

References

U.S. Department of Labor, Manpower Administration, *Merchandising Your Job Talents,* 1971.
U.S. Department of Labor, Women's Bureau, *Job Finding Techniques for Mature Women,* 1970.
U.S. Department of Labor, Women's Bureau, *The Myth and the Reality,* 1971.
"Working in the '70's," *Mademoiselle* magazine, January 1974.

CHAPTER VII

What to Expect in the Workplace

Moving from school or training into the world of full-time work is a major life change. Although you probably will not feel as bewildered at the workplace as Alice did in Wonderland, you may initially feel that you have fallen through a rabbit hole into a strange new land.

Unless you work within a school, your first job will take you to physical surroundings much different from the classrooms you have known since childhood. You will meet strangers who will become your co-workers—including one who will be your boss— and these unknown people may talk "shop talk" you do not understand at first or use unfamiliar job-related jargon. Perhaps most important, you will be faced with work-related responsibilities, rewards, and opportunities different from those you knew as a student.

It will take some time for you to "learn the ropes" of your first job. You may be able to speed up the transition from student to working woman, however, by learning in advance what the work world will expect from you and what you can expect from it.

Responsibilities

When you accept any job, you make a contract with an employer; you agree to perform certain duties in return for a specified

136

number of dollars and other benefits. In line with this agreement, your foremost work responsibility is to do the tasks you were hired to do in the way and at the time that your employer wants them done.

Suppose you are a secretary, for example, and your boss directs you to type several letters and have them ready for signature "by close of business." Your job will then be to type the letters, address an envelope for each, make sure both are free of errors, and present the completed letters to the boss before quitting time. You will also be responsible for doing these tasks in the way your office prescribes. For instance, you may need to type the letters with two-inch side margins, make three carbon copies of each, and arrange the letters, copies, and envelopes in a folder that you give to the boss.

Fail to do this assignment correctly or on time and you are likely to be criticized. Employers differ in their willingness to tolerate work they judge below par, but most have competency standards their employees must meet. Employees whose work frequently or consistently falls below these standards risk being fired for failing to keep up their end of the employment bargain.

Besides being expected to do competently the work for which you are being paid, you will probably also be responsible for being at work regularly unless you are sick or have some other legitimate reason for being absent. Workers who do not appear because they simply did not feel like working or had difficulty in getting out of bed do not have legitimate reasons for absence.

Employers usually want workers who must be absent to notify their bosses or co-workers as soon as possible. You may be instructed to telephone your workplace at—or even before—starting time to explain if you will be absent because of illness. Workers who anticipate that they will need to miss work on a particular day are generally expected to let their supervisors know as far in advance as possible. If you feel sick one afternoon and expect to be absent the next day, for example, you should tell your boss that afternoon that you probably will be out the next day. The same applies if you must take time from work for a doctor's appointment or to conduct banking or legal business that you cannot take care of outside of work hours.

Employers have good reasons for wanting workers to be on the job regularly. Important tasks may not get done if a worker is not there to do them, or other workers may be pressed into taking on extra work so that a job is completed. Moreover, in factories and some other workplaces where work is done by a coordinated team of employees, work activity may slow down or stop altogether if too many people are absent.

Many employers are rigorous about punctuality for many of the same reasons they expect regular attendance. Workplaces that are open for business between specified hours must have workers there between those times to answer telephones, deal with customers, and carry on work activities. An employer's work output, profits, and public image may all suffer if workers are not on hand to take care of business during business hours. Employers therefore expect workers to be ready to work at starting time, to stay until quitting time, and to take no more than the allotted time for lunch periods or coffee breaks. Workers who are unavoidably late for work are often expected to telephone their workplaces at or before starting time to let their co-workers know when they will arrive.

Many workers pay a price for missing work, arriving late or leaving early, or overstaying their lunch periods; they are not paid for the time they miss. (Some organizations, particularly those employing white-collar workers, have sick leave and vacation plans that allow employees to be absent from work for a specified number of days or hours each year and still receive pay for the time they miss.) In addition, many employers view irregular work

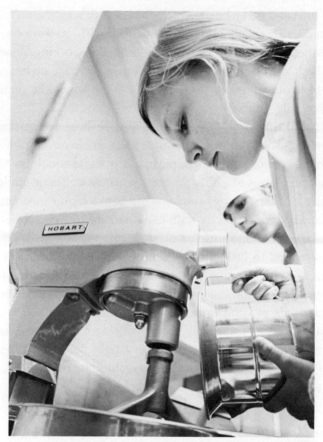

COURTESY U.S. DEPARTMENT OF LABOR

Employers generally expect workers to attend work regularly and to arrive on time. Operations like the institutional food preparation shown here— can slow down or stop altogether if too many workers are absent.

attendance, habitual lateness, or abuse of lunch or coffee-break time policies as grounds for dismissal.

Besides having the responsibility for being on the job during work hours, you will probably also be expected to work during those times. Many employers refuse to put up with employees who waste time and tie up business telephones with lengthy or frequent personal calls, spend much time visiting with co-workers, read newspapers or magazines when they should be working, disappear from their desks or work stations during the day, or find other ways to waste company time. "Goof off" in ways like these and you may find yourself out of a job.

As a full-time worker, you may also be held responsible for maintaining the kind of appearance your employer considers acceptable. Some organizations, particularly those which try to present specific kinds of public images, set dress codes or guidelines for their workers. For example, some banks require women employees who work directly with bank patrons to wear rather conservative clothes and little or no makeup, and firms whose business is related to fashion may expect female employees to wear the latest styles. Even where no official dress policies exist, employers may assume that workers will dress in accordance with the standards of good taste prevailing in the organization. Such standards vary considerably from workplace to workplace, but "party clothes," clothing that is very tight-fitting or revealing, garish makeup, and dirty or sloppy clothing or hairstyles are generally taboo.

Personal Attitudes

Besides setting standards for work performance, attendance, and appearance, employers often hold workers responsible for demonstrating a number of personal traits and attitudes on the job.

Take your work seriously. This means taking full responsibility for the work you do, showing interest in your duties, performing to the best of your ability, and asking questions if you do not understand exactly what you are supposed to do. (If you choose an occupation and an employer wisely, you will probably meet these expectations naturally because you are interested in your work and want to do it well.) Employers do not welcome employees who do slipshod work, show obvious lack of interest in their jobs, try to wiggle out of assignments, act resentful or angry when they are given work to do, or try to pass the buck for their mistakes.

Keep your mind on your job. As a worker, you will be expected to concentrate on the work at hand rather than daydreaming about your boyfriend, trying to decide what color to paint the walls in your apartment, or thinking about your husband or children. It is often difficult to put aside important personal concerns, but it is to your benefit to learn to focus on your job during working hours. In the first place, you are likely to do better work when you concentrate than when you are distracted by other thoughts. You are also apt to find that you are more interested and absorbed in your work if you give it your full attention.

Keep this employer expectation in mind if you find yourself interested in turning work relationships with men into personal relationships. Men do outnumber women in the work world, and you may well be attracted to men you meet through work. Before plunging into a romance with a male co-worker, however, you may want to consider the practical problems that may result. Suppose, for example, that you must work closely with a man you date. Your work relationship could suffer if you become too starry-eyed about each other to keep your minds on business, or, on the other hand, if your personal relationship hits snags that make it awkward or uncomfortable for you to work together. And even if you do not work directly with a man you become involved with, you may need to see him every day on the job no matter how well or badly your relationship is going. It makes sense to consider in advance whether you could handle this type of situation without being distracted from your work or suffering too many bad feelings.

Be honest. Most employers object strenuously when people whose salaries they pay steal from them. Under the law, taking home a few of the employer's office supplies is no less an act of stealing than is shoplifting. Stealing is a serious problem in the work world, particularly in the retail, manufacturing, and transport industries, and employers are increasingly taking a hard line against offenders by prosecuting or firing them, or both.

In a related issue of honesty, employers also expect that workers will not use company equipment, supplies, or information for their personal advantage or in ways that could hurt the employer. Helping competitors and misusing information to which you have access because of your position within an organization may be grounds for discharge or other penalties. Inasmuch as most employers value loyalty, they also expect workers to refrain from maliciously gossiping or make derogatory comments about the employer, especially to persons outside the organization.

Be courteous and cooperative in dealings with co-workers, clients, and other work contacts. Many employers look with disfavor on workers who gossip about or indulge in petty feuds with their co-workers, treat co-workers or customers rudely, or let their feelings interfere with their ability to be fair and impartial in work relationships. Such actions cut down on a worker's effectiveness and may hurt the employer's profits or public image.

Be willing and able to accept constructive criticism. Because of old myths about the characteristics of women, some employers are afraid women workers will burst into tears at the least bit of criticism. Because no worker is perfect and employers frequently need to offer criticism, they may limit opportunities for women in order to avoid this problem.

It is not true, of course, that all women react poorly to criticism, but some, like some men, certainly do. If you are among those who find it difficult to accept criticism, try to remember that errors are an inevitable part of living and that criticism that helps you to become more competent is to your advantage. You might also remind yourself that it is only a tiny portion of your lifetime work that is under fire, not your overall abilities, or your worth and value as a human being. Remember, too, that reacting angrily or with hurt feelings to legitimate criticism may harm your chances for job advancement as well as reinforce the already unfavorable attitude some employers have toward women workers.

Obligations of the Employer

As a working woman, you will need to meet most—if not all—of your employer's expectations in order to keep your job or to move up. On the other side of the coin, you will also have a right to expect your employer to fulfill various obligations to you.

For example, you may hold your employer responsible for letting you know exactly what is expected of you on the job and for giving you the instructions, training, and guidance you need in order to meet these expectations. Providing this type of assistance is generally the job of your immediate boss or supervisor. You will probably report to your supervisor on your first day at work, and he or she will most likely show you to your desk or work station, introduce you to your co-workers, and help you learn your way around the workplace. In time, he or she should explain precisely what your duties are, see that you get the instructions and materials you need to perform your work adequately, outline the work rules and procedures you will be expected to follow, and tell you what penalties can be placed on you if you fail to meet your work obligations.

Large organizations often conduct orientation sessions that supplement the information new employees get from their supervisors. Such programs are often run by people from the personnel department, the unit in charge of hiring and training, labor relations, payroll functions, administration of promotion and job-transfer policies, and related matters.

Orientation sessions typically give new workers background information about the employer, explain the kinds of work done by different units within the organization, and show how these units are related. They may also outline the organization's work rules, describe pay and other worker benefits, explain how employees' work and progress are evaluated, describe promotion policies, explain the role of the union within the organization, tell workers whom to contact if they have difficulty working with their supervisors or are unhappy on the job, and offer other useful information that helps workers understand how the agency operates and where they fit into the picture.

As you settle into your job, your immediate supervisor will have day-to-day responsibility for giving you assignments, assessing your work, offering constructive criticism when necessary, and letting you know if your progress is satisfactory, more than adequate, or below par. Should you feel your supervisor is not meeting his or her responsibilities in these areas (suppose you are receiving vague or incomplete instructions, for example, or being expected to conform to work rules that were never explained to you), you should discuss the matter with your supervisor and tactfully let him or her know that the two of you are not communicating effectively. If you cannot iron out the problems this way, you may want to consult an appropriate person from the personnel office, your supervisor's supervisor, or, in unionized organizations, a union representative.

Besides expecting your supervisor to give you the specific information you need to do your job, you can also expect him or her to give you that information courteously. The same rules that govern human relationships apply to working relationships; you are entitled to be treated fairly and with dignity, respect, and courtesy on the job as well as off. Supervisors who grant "pet" workers special privileges they deny others, insult or abuse workers, or use their power to prevent workers they dislike from getting promotions or other rewards they deserve are not meeting their obligation to treat employees as human beings as well as workers. You will be perfectly justified in complaining to higher authorities about such abuses of power and position.

One of your employer's foremost responsibilities will be to pay you for your work. You may be paid once a week, once every two weeks, on specified days (say the first and fifteenth of each month), or according to some other schedule. No matter how often you are paid, however, you can expect your employer to withhold certain amounts from your base pay.

Under the law, employers must withhold money from your pay for federal and, in most states, state income taxes. The amount withheld will depend upon the amount you earn, the number of persons you support (such people are called "dependents"), the tax laws in your state, and other factors. If you are single with no dependents except yourself and earn $150 a week, you can expect to have about $24 a week withheld for federal taxes and another $8 or so for state taxes. When you begin work, you will fill out tax withholding forms indicating your marital status and the number of your dependents. This information should enable your employer to withhold enough money from each paycheck to cover your yearly tax bill.

If you work for the federal government, your agency will also withhold money for the federal employees' retirement program. Otherwise, money will probably be withheld for the Social Security program. By law, most workers must participate in these plans, which entitle you to receive retirement pay and other benefits. You may also elect to have money withheld from your pay for a hospitalization plan, life insurance, a pension plan, or other employee-benefit programs for which you and your employer share the costs.

The retirement pay, hospitalization coverage, and other benefits you receive from plans to which your employer contributes money are called fringe benefits. Because fringe benefits can raise your total income by a significant amount, it is to your advantage to learn as much as you can about such plans and to take part in those which offer worthwhile benefits. Your supervisor, personnel department, or payroll office should be able to provide details about such plans.

Laws Concerning Employment of Women

Besides being obligated to obey laws concerning employee tax withholdings and retirement plans, employers must also adhere to a variety of other federal and state regulations designed to protect the rights of workers. These include laws that set hourly minimum wages for certain workers and require that such workers be paid extra for overtime work, protect employees' rights to take part or to refrain from taking part in union activities, and protect workers from many occupational safety and health hazards. Other laws make it illegal for employers to discriminate against workers solely on the basis of their sex. As a working woman, you should be aware of all these laws and expect employers to obey them, but you may want to become especially familiar with the provisions of laws that protect women's rights in the work world.

One of the most important of these laws is the Federal Civil Rights Act of 1964. This law prohibits discrimination because of race, color, religion, sex, or national origin in hiring, promotions, training, and all other conditions of employment.

Under this law, which is administered by the U. S. Equal Employment Opportunity Commission, located in Washington, D.C., all jobs must be open to both men and women unless an employer can prove that sex "is a bona fide occupational qualification reasonably necessary to the normal operation of that particular business or enterprise." Under this guideline, jobs may be restricted to members of one sex only for reasons of authenticity (actress, actor, model); because of community standards or morality or propriety (restroom attendant, lingerie salesclerk); and in jobs in the entertainment industry in which sex appeal is an essential qualification.

Jobs may not be restricted to members of one sex for any of the following reasons:

1. Job applicants of one sex are assumed to possess certain attitudes. For example, a job cannot be reserved for men because an employer believes that women are unable or unwilling to do that job.

2. Co-workers, employers, clients, or customers prefer one sex over the other.

3. The job has traditionally been restricted to members of the opposite sex.

4. The job involves heavy physical labor, manual dexterity, late-night hours, overtime, work in isolated locations, or work in unpleasant surroundings.

5. The job involves travel, or travel with members of the opposite sex.

6. Physical facilities are not available for both sexes. This can be used as an excuse only in cases where the cost of providing additional facilities is extremely high.

7. The job requires personal characteristics believed to belong only to one sex. Examples of such traits might be tact, charm, or aggressiveness.

In line with these regulations, help-wanted advertisements may not specify any preference for workers of a certain sex or any limitations applying to workers of one sex unless sex is a legitimate occupational qualification. Want ads may not specify that jobs are open only to men or to women, nor may ads be placed in separate columns headed "Help Wanted—Female" or "Help Wanted—Male."

Besides outlawing discrimination based on sex in the hiring of workers, the Civil Rights Act also prohibits such discrimination in all conditions of employment. In other words, all employees, whether men or women, are entitled to equal treatment with regard to recruitment, hiring, layoffs, discharges, and recalls; opportunities for promotions; opportunities to participate in training programs; wages and salaries; sick-leave time and pay; medical, hospital, life, and accident insurance coverage; qualifications for retirement and pension benefits; and rest periods, coffee breaks, lunch periods, and smoking breaks.

(With respect to maternity leave, which of course applies only to women, the Equal Employment Opportunity Commission has said that female workers are entitled to a leave of absence for childbearing, and that employers may require pregnant women to take leave ninety days before their due date.)

The sex discrimination provisions of the Civil Rights Act apply to employers of twenty-five or more persons, except for government agencies and private educational institutions. The law also applies to unions with twenty-five or more members, unions that operate hiring halls, and employment agencies dealing with employers of twenty-five or more people.

If you ever feel you have been discriminated against in a work situation on the basis of sex, you may file a discrimination charge with the U.S. Equal Employment Opportunity Commission, 1800 G Street, N.W., Washington, D.C. 20506. The commission can provide instructions, complaint forms, and legal advice. Do not be afraid to file a charge because you think your employer might make life difficult for you. It is unlawful for any employer, employment agency, or union to punish you for filing a complaint or speaking out against practices that are illegal under this law.

Other laws make it illegal for federal agencies and most companies that hold contracts or subcontracts with the federal government to discriminate on the basis of sex. These employers must also establish programs, known as affirmative action programs, that are designed to insure that workers are hired without regard to sex.

Another federal law that protects your right to equal treatment on the job is the Equal Pay Act, passed by Congress in 1963. This law makes it illegal for employers to pay workers of one sex less than they pay workers of the opposite sex for doing equal work in jobs that require substantially equal skills, effort, and responsibility and that are done under similar working conditions. This law applies to overtime pay and employer contributions to employee-benefit plans as well as to pay.

The Equal Pay Act also makes it illegal for employers to reduce the amount they pay workers of one sex in order to comply with the law. Further information about this act is available from the Wage and Hour Division, Employment Standards Administration, U.S. Department of Labor, Washington, D.C. 20210. You may also write to this agency to report violations of the law.

Many state and local governments have also enacted laws forbidding sex discrimination in employment. For information about such laws, contact your state or local fair employment practices commission, listed in the white pages of your telephone directory under state, city, or county government listings.

References

Kimbell, Grady and Ben S. Vineyard, *Succeeding in the World of Work,* McKnight & McKnight Publishing Company, Bloomington, Ill., 1970.

U.S. Department of Labor, Women's Bureau, *Laws on Sex Discrimination in Employment,* 1973.

U.S. Equal Employment Opportunity Commission, *Toward Job Equality for Women,* 1969.

CHAPTER VIII

Moving Up

During the first stages of your work life, you will stand at or near the bottom of the career ladder in your field. From that position, you will probably see workers at higher levels who are earning more money than you, working out of more private or attractive quarters, doing work that is more varied or challenging than yours, having more say in workplace decisions, and enjoying greater prestige and recognition. These are the rewards of job advancement, and these benefits may encourage you to try to move up in the work world.

Advantages and Disadvantages

Purely economic motives may spur you to seek some promotions and the higher pay that accompanies them. Your expenses —and hence your income needs—will probably grow during your work life as you try to keep ahead of rising prices, furnish a house or apartment, and develop tastes for travel, more expensive clothing, or the other pleasures that money can buy. Pay raises may be especially important if you become a working mother, because the costs of rearing a child increase substantially with the child's growth from infancy to college age.

You may also want to move up in the work world to gain the personal rewards of advancement. Work variety is one such reward. Stand on one rung of the job ladder for very long and you are apt to find yourself doing the same tasks or the same kind of work over and over. If you find such repetition boring, you may welcome a move up to a position in which you can learn new skills and assume new assignments.

Advancement will also be important if you want your work to offer continuing chances to meet new challenges, make increasing contributions to your field, assume greater responsibilities, or grow in other ways. And inasmuch as promotions are a sign of recognition for past work well done and a mark of confidence in your ability to take on more challenging duties, they can give you the pleasure of an "ego boost" as well.

But job advancement may have drawbacks as well as benefits. For example, workers in some fields can advance to top pay and responsibility levels only by assuming supervisory or management jobs. Thus, teachers who want maximum pay and decision-making authority must usually become school administrators, many writers must become editors if they want to advance, and secretaries may need to become office managers. Workers who move up in these ways may oversee the work of others or make decisions about work methods and priorities, but have little opportunity to do the kind of work they did previously, the work that may have attracted them to their occupations in the first place. And not all workers enjoy or do well at supervisory or management jobs; a good teacher may far prefer classroom work to administrative chores but be unable to gain the income, power, or prestige he or she wants by remaining a teacher.

Workers in supervisory and management jobs often need to put in longer workdays or workweeks than their subordinates, too, and spending more time at work means having less time for other activities. This kind of trade-off is unacceptable to many workers who do not want their jobs to infringe on the time they spend with their families or in off-the-job activities they enjoy.

Women who advance to managerial and supervisory jobs often need to work longer and harder than their subordinates. Many women, however, thoroughly enjoy these challenges, responsibility, pay, and recognition.

Moreover, the increased responsibilities and challenges that are the earmarks of job advancement often bring new work pressures and risks. The higher up the ladder you climb, the more decisions you will probably need to make, the more impact those decisions will have, and the more chances you will have to err.

Workers who must vie with others for promotions may find the competition uncomfortable or even unpleasant. There is usually little room at the top of any organization, and in some fields and offices, the struggle for top-level positions is fierce. Workers who want to move up the ladder under such circumstances may need to be able to keep their footing as co-workers try to block the way or even to push them off balance.

Although you are apt to start work with some knowledge of the possibilities for advancement, you will learn more about the opportunities open to you and the costs of moving up in your field as you gain work experience. In deciding how far up the ladder you want to climb, you will need to weigh the benefits of upward movement against the disadvantages, using your own needs, interests, and ambitions as a scale. If the balance tips in favor of seeking advancement, do not be afraid to aim as high as you want.

Some women are reluctant to set their sights on top-level jobs because they fear others will think them "unfeminine." Some hesitate because they think job success will cut down on their chances of marrying; they believe that men are not interested in successful women.

Such hesitations are based on traditional notions about a woman's role and do not take into account the uniqueness or needs of individual women. If moving up gives you satisfaction, increases your self-esteem, or puts you in a position to make the kind of contribution you want to make to your field, why hold back because of what others may think about your "femininity"? Girls who fear that success will interfere with their chances of marriage should remember that just as some boys like girls who do well in school, so some men enjoy successful working women, share their interests and values, and admire their competence and drive.

Looking for Advancement

No matter how far up the ladder you aim to go, your chances of reaching your goal will be influenced by several variables, including the opportunities for advancement within your occupation and with your employer. That is why it is important to explore advancement opportunities before choosing an occupation or taking a job.

Your knowledge of the routes to advancement will also be important. Many employing agencies, particularly larger ones, have clear-cut promotion policies. For example, employees may need to hold one job for a certain amount of time before they are eligible to be promoted. In some companies, employees who wish to be considered for higher-level positions must apply formally for them, while in others, supervisors approach employees with promotion offers. You will need to know exactly what promotion procedures exist in your organization in order to take effective steps toward moving up.

Find out, too, whether any unofficial routes to higher jobs exist within your organization. In many employing agencies, some people in the chain of command wield more power or influence than others, even if this influence is not indicated by their titles or positions. For example, in a company where the lowest-level employees are supervised by a dozen managers who report to three vice-presidents who work under the top executive, a few of the twelve middle-level managers and at least one of the vice-presidents are apt—because of their skills, personalities, backgrounds, contacts, or some other assets—to be a little more influential than others at the same level. If such differences affect decisions about promotions, it is to your advantage to know whose opinions carry the most weight. (You can often figure this out by seeing which departments are growing fastest, which have the largest budgets, and which officials are looked on most favorably by higher-level executives.) You need not defer unduly to these officials, of course, but it may be to your advantage to have them know you and your work.

COURTESY U.S. DEPARTMENT OF LABOR

Some occupations offer relatively few chances for advancement. Unless she becomes a supervisor, for example, the electronics assembly worker shown here is likely to have little opportunity to learn new skills, take on decision-making responsibilities, or move to a higher pay scale.

Besides knowing what kinds of promotions are available and how one goes about getting them, you will also need to qualify for higher positions if you want to advance. The foremost qualification is usually competence. Most employers will not give you a chance to move to the second rung on the ladder until you show your ability to do first-rung tasks.

To many employers, a good work attitude is as important a qualification as good work performance. Such employers may reserve promotions for people who follow rules about punctuality and attendance, show interest in their work and loyalty toward the employing organization, treat clients or customers courteously, show initiative by taking on work that must be done without waiting to be told, get along well with co-workers at all levels, or demonstrate other valued traits.

You may also need to have a specific amount or kind of education or training in order to qualify for promotions. If you lack such preparation, you may be able to learn needed skills or prepare for supervisory or management jobs through training programs set up by your employer. Many employers are also willing to pay all or part of the costs of college courses or other educational or training programs related to an employee's work. Your supervisor or personnel office will have details about such arrangements.

Should neither of these options be available, you might enroll in classes at a college, community college, or technical school during your off-work hours, or take appropriate correspondence courses. If you consider taking such courses solely in the hopes that they will help you get ahead, however, make sure they are actually likely to help you meet your goals before you pay tuition or fees. Your supervisor or a personnel office representative should be able to help you determine whether specific courses will enhance your chances of moving up.

A record of competence and the qualifications for higher-level work are usually necessary for advancement, but they may not be sufficient for advancement. An unfortunate fact of work life is that promotions do not always go to workers who deserve them.

For example, employers sometimes do not promote workers who are performing well because they would then need to spend time, energy, and money in finding and training a replacement. Rather than face these expenses, employers may prefer to fill vacancies with workers from outside the department or agency instead of by promoting persons already employed in the unit. Seniority—length of service on the job in relation to that of other workers—may also come into play. Promotions in some organizations are based at least partly on seniority, and in such situations, workers with the most experience may be promoted before more able workers with less time on the job. Sometimes, too, promotions are based on friendship or political considerations rather than solely on merit.

More important for working women seeking advancement, however, is the fact that some employers are reluctant to promote women beyond certain levels no matter how competent those women are. This attitude may be based on the belief that women are not emotionally or mentally equipped to perform supervisory jobs or those which demand responsible decision-making, interactions with male clients or customers, travel, or other activities that have come to be considered more suitable for men than for women. Refusing to promote a woman simply because of her sex or because of notions like the ones above is illegal under the sex discrimination provisions of the federal Civil Rights Act, but employers with these viewpoints sometimes still find ways to promote men rather than equally or better qualified women.

Some employers are reluctant to promote women to supervisory jobs because they think neither men nor women want to work for women supervisors. Like most other generalities, this one fails to take into account the differences between individuals. It also ignores the fact that many men and women who have worked under the supervision of capable women have enjoyed working for them.

Another myth some employers operate under when making promotions is the idea that women do not want responsible positions but prefer to remain in relatively low-level jobs. Yet some women, like some men, welcome—even thrive on—upward movement, whereas others of both sexes choose not to climb career ladders.

As a working woman interested in advancement, you may need to take positive action to overcome such stereotypes and prejudices. Promote yourself as a candidate for promotions; become your own best salesperson.

One way to increase your chance of advancing is by letting people in your organization who make decisions about promotions know that you are doing a good job and that you are interested in moving up. You may need to tell your supervisor of your aims directly, or you may need to make other appropriate officials aware of you and your work. To do the latter, you might serve on work-related committees or take part in other activities that give you an opportunity to work with people in positions of authority. Another possibility is to join trade associations, professional organizations, or employee groups in which you can make contact with higher-level men and women and talk with them about your work. Or you might take on extra duties such as speaking to school or community groups about your work or teaching a course in your field. People in decision-making positions are likely to hear of such activities and recognize them as signs of your ability, interest, and initiative.

As part of your advancement campaign, particularly on your first job or in your first several jobs, you may need to convince your superiors that you are not simply "a nice girl" or "a sweet young thing"—the labels that men and older workers sometimes put on young working women—but a serious contender for promotions. Do your work well, keep up with new developments in your organization and in your field, show good judgment and the ability to make sound decisions, learn "to keep your cool" under pressure or when facing criticism, make useful suggestions for improving work methods, speak up at staff meetings, and do whatever else you can to show interest in and commitment to your work.

It may also be worthwhile to develop the ability to speak clearly, succinctly, and matter-of-factly. Many girls and women speak too softly or hesitantly and smile even when smiles are inappropriate. Such mannerisms detract from a woman's effectiveness in work situations and may give others the impression that she is unbusinesslike or less capable than she really is.

You may also want to dress in a manner that suggests competence and strength rather than one that emphasizes youth, daintiness, or frivolousness. You probably will want to look attractive, of course, because attractiveness is—for both men and women —an undeniable asset in the work world.

Recognizing that attractiveness is an asset does not mean using sex as a means to advancement, however, even though women sometimes think their chances of moving up will be greater if they flirt or sleep with men who make promotion decisions. Should you ever think of using sex as a stepping stone, you might ask yourself these questions: Will you really move up if you flirt or sleep with the boss? Some men suggest that this will be the case, but never deliver the promotions. Regardless of whether or not you are promoted, will you feel comfortable about continuing to work with any man involved? Is your involvement likely to be known by others in your work group and, if so, will you feel uncomfortable? Will your actions affect attitudes toward working women as a group? And perhaps most important, will you feel good about yourself if you use sex as a means of advancement?

But what if you do your best to get a promotion that goes to someone else? A long, hard look at yourself and your work situation is then in order. Were you really well qualified for the position you wanted? Was the person who got the position you wanted more qualified by virtue of work performance, preparation, or experience? Was the promotion made strictly on the basis of merit, or were other considerations important?

This kind of examination may help you learn how you can take more effective steps toward advancement next time. For example, you may find that you need to become better qualified or to work harder at seeking promotions. On the other hand, you may discover that you missed out on the promotion for reasons that had nothing to do with your qualifications. For example, you may see good evidence that you were discriminated against because you are a woman. If so, you may want to file a complaint with the appropriate government agency.

Should your analysis suggest that your chances of moving up in the organization are, for whatever reason, poor, you may need to move to a different department within your organization or to find another job where your chances of moving up will be brighter.

In summary, the keys to moving up are to decide where you want to go and to do what you must in order to get there. It is not enough to do your work well in the hopes that employers will come to you with promotion offers. This is akin to sitting at a drugstore soda fountain waiting for a producer or director to "discover" you and make you a star. One or two movie stars have started in this way, but the great majority of actors and actresses must audition for roles that may lead to stardom. In short, they must sell themselves and their talents, and you will need to do the same in order to get ahead.

References

Dunlap, Jan, *Personal and Professional Success for Women,* Prentice-Hall, Inc., Englewood Cliffs, 1972.

Kimbrell, Grady and Ben S. Vineyard, *Succeeding in the World of Work,* McKnight & McKnight Publishing Company, Bloomington, Ill., 1970.

CHAPTER IX

Combining Work and Family

Gardeners who want to enjoy their flowers throughout the growing season often plant several varieties that bloom at different times of the year. They might choose, say, tulips to enjoy in the spring, summer roses, and chrysanthemums that bloom in the fall.

A variety of satisfactions may blossom at different times during a woman's life, too. Among these are the joys of marriage and motherhood. Girls who want to enjoy their lives to the fullest need to learn about the pleasures and responsibilities of love and family relationships as well as those of work. This information can help you decide what mix of life activities might be most satisfying for you.

If You Marry

Many of the satisfactions of work were outlined in the first chapter of this book. They include money, mental stimulation, the chance to contribute to society, interaction with people who share your work interests, avenues for self-expression and recognition, and feelings of independence, competence, and strength.

Marriage can offer the emotional satisfactions that may come from a close, loving relationship with a man. Marital pleasures can include comfortable companionship and the bonds formed when two people share both the joys and sorrows of day-to-day life. Building a home together, sharing common interests and goals, living with a good friend—these can also be gratifying.

Contrary to many girls' expectations, however, marriage is not a haven from the problems and demands of life. Like single women, married women must make most of their own important life decisions, set and live by their own values, and meet most of their own needs if they are to achieve whatever will make them happiest in life. The woman who believes that marriage will rescue her from the need to stand on her own two feet most of the time or who thinks her husband will take care of her as a parent cares for a child is apt to be disappointed.

Divorce statistics show that a great many marriages end less than happily and long before "ever after." Moreover, the going is sometimes rough even in the best of marriages, and getting through such times may take a lot of hard work. Ability to reach and accept compromise, willingness to consider another person's point of view, commitment, patience, and a sense of humor are tremendous assets to any man and woman who attempt to live together.

The emotional pleasures of love and sharing that can occur in marriage are also possible in motherhood. In addition, mothers can derive a great deal of satisfaction from caring for children, watching them grow, helping them learn, playing with them, and learning from them how to see the world through a child's eyes.

Like marriage, rearing a child takes patience, commitment, and willingness to consider others' needs and feelings. It also requires a great deal of time; a multitude of chores are involved in feeding, housing, and clothing children, looking out for their well-being, and doing the countless other tasks they cannot do for themselves.

Although most women currently do marry and bear children, you are not obliged to choose these life activities any more than a gardener is obliged to grow any specific kind of plant. Some women choose to forego marriage and raising a family because of the hard work and strong commitment they require, or because they feel that a husband or children would interfere with the kind of life-styles they wish to lead, unduly hamper their independence and freedom, or present other disadvantages. Strong social pressures are placed on women to marry and bear children, but you are nevertheless free to choose whatever mix of life activities you prefer. Your own personality, interests, needs, and life goals offer the best guides to determining whether or not marriage and motherhood would be satisfying for you.

If you do look forward to taking on the roles of wife and mother sometime during your life, you might want to explore ways of combining these roles with full- or part-time work. You then can anticipate some of the issues that may arise.

A good many married women work full time, particularly during the early years of marriage and again after their children are somewhat self-sufficient. It takes some juggling, however, to combine marriage and work responsibilities in a way that maximizes a woman's enjoyment of both roles while minimizing potential conflicts and pressures.

Although some working wives are married to "househusbands" who do not work outside the home, to students, or to men who work part time, a large number are married to men who work full time. In the latter situation, both members of a couple need to understand the importance of each person's work in his or her own life and in their life together, for such understanding provides a basis for making mutually agreeable decisions related to their work and income. Consider the following questions: Will a couple move to a different location if the husband is offered a better job there? Will they move if the wife is offered a transfer that involves a promotion? Will they move only if both partners can find satisfying jobs in the new location? The decision is likely to be based on the importance the couple attaches to each partner's work and

COURTESY U.S. DEPARTMENT OF LABOR

Many women choose not to work while their children are young, but others work part or full time. The mother's interests, skills, values, energies, financial circumstances, and ability to make child-care arrangements are likely to figure in work decisions.

income as well as on the income gains or other benefits that may result.

Working couples need to make some decisions about family income and spending, too. Will they put both paychecks into a common pool that will cover household purchases, savings, vacations, clothes for each, or whatever else they want? Will each partner chip in part of his or her income to cover joint expenses and keep the remainder to spend however he or she wishes? Will one person's income be used for living expenses and the other paycheck saved or invested? Will the couple have a joint checking account or separate accounts?

You can prepare now to make decisions like these by trying to find out what type of work and financial arrangements you are likely to feel most comfortable with if you become a working wife. Will you want your career to be considered as important as your husband's, will you want him to assume the traditional role of "breadwinner," or can you foresee your income as the one you and your husband consider the primary one? Are you likely to want to retain some of your income for purely personal use, or will you prefer to put your paycheck into a common pot? How do you think you and your husband should make decisions about what to purchase, how much to spend for a particular item, or how to manage your money? By considering questions like these, you can begin to learn what roles work and money are likely to play in your married life and use this information in making future decisions.

Who Does the Chores?

Provisions for taking care of household chores also need to be made when both a husband and wife work. (You may need to do household chores as a single working woman, of course, but managing a household for two is a bit more complicated than homemaking for one because you need to take another person's opinions and desires into account. Nevertheless, some of the suggestions below may be useful to single working women as well as to those who marry.)

Traditionally, women have been responsible for doing household tasks within marriage, but other arrangements are possible.

You and your husband can each do half the chores. You might try to divide the work so that each of you does the tasks you enjoy most (or dislike least), or you might split them on the basis of convenience or efficiency. For example, you might decide that the person who gets home from work first will cook dinner.

If you can afford it, you and your husband may hire a maid or other private household worker to do some chores.

One of you may assume overall responsibility for doing the housework. The other may help out, or you might hire someone to take care of some tasks.

Whatever arrangement you adopt should be agreeable to both partners. Tensions and resentments are likely to arise if one of you thinks you are shouldering too much of the load or feels that the arrangement is in some other way inadequate or unfair. Your arrangement will need to take into account the "messiness tolerance" of each individual, too, for the amount of order or disorder people feel comfortable with varies from person to person.

Because time is important to people who combine homemaking and paid employment, you might choose to minimize the time required for household tasks by eliminating those you regard as unnecessary—making beds, say, or waxing furniture. If your budget allows, you might also eat out as often as possible, have a laundry wash your clothes, or pay for other conveniences that will give you more time to relax and enjoy leisure interests.

If You Become a Mother

Combining the roles of mother and working woman is more difficult than juggling those of wife and working woman. Child care is a major responsibility, and many women choose not to work during the time their children are young in order to enjoy to the fullest the pleasures of motherhood or because they feel that children need a mother's full-time attention during the early years.

Some women who devote all their time to the time-consuming but often routine tasks of caring for children and a home feel bored, trapped, and lonely. They may long for adult companionship during the day, crave the mental stimulation or feelings of accomplishment available through paid employment, miss the financial independence that accompanies a paycheck, and lose self-confidence and self-esteem. Mothers with such feelings often choose to work either part or full time.

To decide whether or not you might want to combine work and motherhood, ask yourself the following questions.

1. Do you believe that children need a mother's full-time attention? Why or why not? If you are convinced that the presence of a mother who does not work outside the home is important to a child's well-being, you are apt to feel guilty about working even part time if you have young children.

2. Do you think you would be a loving, patient mother if you took care of children full time, or are you apt to need outside interests or accomplishments in order to maintain your self-esteem and your ability to give yourself generously to your children?

3. Are you likely to become bored or lonely if you do not work? If so, it may be wise to work at least part time.

4. Do you enjoy good health and abundant energy? Mothers who combine work and family obligations need both. Suppose, for example, that you become a working mother with two children, ages 2 and 5. In the morning, you need to wake the children, dress one and help dress the other, feed them breakfast, drive one to a day-care center and the other to kindergarten, get ready for work, and arrive at your workplace on time ready to do your job.

After work, you need to go home with enough pep to talk or play with your children, do other motherly tasks, and perform some household chores. The need for good health and energy becomes obvious. (So does the need to set aside some time to relax. Working mothers need rest and recreation activities in order to refresh themselves for their double-duty life.)

5. Can you organize your time and activities efficiently? The example above indicates why working mothers need to make the best possible use of their hours and efforts.

6. Will you be able to give a job the time and concentration it demands? Working mothers who cannot focus on their jobs because of family responsibilities do not live up to their agreements with their employers. Besides jeopardizing a woman's job, such behavior may tarnish even further the unfavorable attitudes some employers hold toward women.

Your financial situation will also be important to your future decisions concerning work and motherhood. Many mothers who are widowed, divorced, separated, or unmarried need to work in order to support their children; and many others want to work in order to raise their family's standard of living. If you consider working strictly for financial reasons, however, look at the real monetary gains your job will provide. The costs of child care and such work-related expenses as commuting, lunches, and clothes can eat up a sizable amount of a working mother's income. The difference between these costs and a mother's income should be great enough to justify her working for monetary reasons.

Your decision about whether or not to become a working mother may also hinge on your ability to make adequate child-care arrangements. Pre-school-age children need care during the workday, and school-age children whose mothers work may need such care before or after school hours. Such care can be provided in a variety of ways. Most working mothers hire individuals to care for children in their own homes or in the baby-sitter's home, but some have relatives who look after the children. Day-care centers and nurseries offer child care, usually for a fee, and a few parents participate in community baby-sitting cooperatives in which several parents either take turns caring for the children or hire someone to look after them. Some husbands and wives whose work schedules differ assume responsibility for child care at different times.

For your own peace of mind and the welfare of your children, be sure that whatever child-care provisions you make offer your children the kind of care you think they need. If child-care arrangements are unsatisfactory, your children may suffer and you may feel guilty about being a "bad mother." If a baby-sitter does not show up regularly, you may also need to take excessive time off from work.

Some emergencies related to child care are apt to arise even under the best of circumstances, however. A baby-sitter may get sick, a day-care center may be closed because of inclement weather, or other problems may crop up. Working mothers can best cope with such emergencies by preparing for them in advance. For example, they might seek out neighbors or relatives who will agree to look after their children in the event that regular child-care arrangements fall through.

If you choose to become a working mother, you will need to determine whether you want to work full or part time. This decision should be based on your financial situation, individual needs and interests, and ability to make child-care arrangements, as well as on your skills and the job opportunities available to you. Should you decide to work full time, you may want to get a job that offers regular hours and tasks you can forget about after work, because it is harder to schedule family responsibilities and child care around jobs that require irregular hours or off-duty attention.

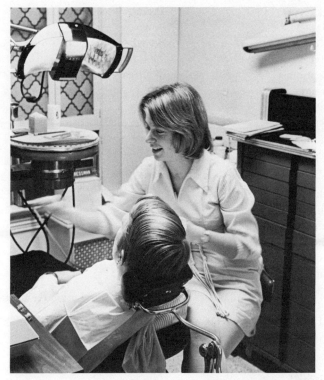

COURTESY G. RICARDO CAMPBELL

Many part-time job opportunities exist for dental hygienists. Girls who think they may want to work part time if they become mothers might explore this aspect of employment when investigating occupations.

Job opportunities for mothers who want to work part time are abundant in many of the fields women have traditionally dominated, but scarce in some nontraditional fields. A good number of part-time opportunities exist in many clerical and service occupations, for example, but relatively few occur in many professional and business occupations. A large number of part-time opportunities are open to the following types of workers:

Bookkeeper
Coder
File clerk
Postal clerk
Receptionist
Secretary
Stenographer
Survey worker
Switchboard operator
Typist

Bank teller
Cashier
Comparison shopper
Demonstrator
Grocery checker
Insurance agent
Market-research
  interviewer
Real estate agent
Travel agent

Bartender
Beautician
Cook
Food-counter attendant
Manicurist

Private household
  worker
Social service aide
Taxi driver
Waitress

College career-planning
  and placement counselor
Home economist
Recreation worker
Teacher (substitute)
Tutor
Social worker
Writer

Dental assistant
Dental hygienist
Dietitian
Electrocardiographic technician
Licensed practical
  nurse
Medical laboratory
  worker
Nursing aide
Occupational therapist
Physical therapist
Registered nurse
X-ray technician

Efforts are currently being made to broaden the number of part-time opportunities in fields that now offer relatively few, and these actions may produce results during the next several years. For example, efforts are being made to increase the number of part-time jobs in the federal government, and a small but growing number of employers in many fields are being persuaded to hire two women to share jobs now done by one full-time worker.

In fields where part-time jobs are rare, employers sometimes allow women with good full-time work records to switch to part-time schedules after they have children. Keep this in mind if you decide to work part time during any stage of your life.

Women with certain skills may also be able to work part time in their own homes. Fields especially well suited to this kind of arrangement include those related to the arts, crafts, and home-making, as well as editing, typing, and writing. Home offices can also be set up by accountants, auditors, lawyers, psychologists, public-relations workers, and some other specialized workers.

Women who work at home generally need self-discipline and a strong desire to work in order to initiate and complete projects without the external pressures of a job, a supervisor, and work hours set by someone else. Inasmuch as phone calls, children, and household emergencies can create distractions, women who work at home also need to find ways to cut down on such interruptions during times they designate as work hours.

If you look forward to motherhood but decide against wearing the hats of mother and working woman at the same time, you should not regard this decision as marking the end of your career. As noted in Chapter I, over half of all women between the ages of 35 and 54 are in the work force, and many of these are women who have returned to work after taking time out for children.

Going Back to Work

You can prepare to reenter the work world by practicing your job skills and keeping in touch with your field during the time you are away from work. Otherwise, your skills are apt to become "rusty" or even obsolete. It may not be easy to keep in touch with your field if home responsibilities are demanding, but there are several ways to do so.

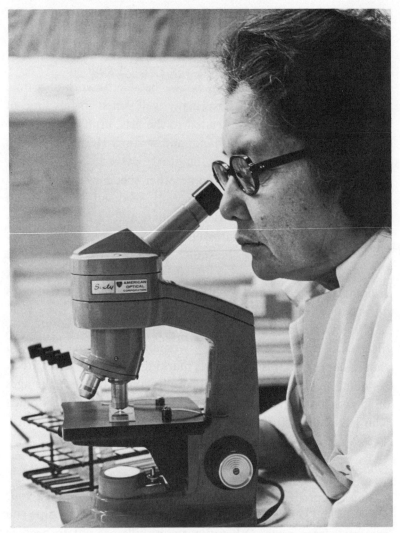

Work techniques in many fields, including laboratory jobs, may change over time as new scientific discoveries are made, new equipment developed, and new data gathered. Women who do not keep up with changes in their fields while they are out of the work force may find that their skills become rusty or obsolete.

1. Keep up membership in professional or trade associations, read trade or technical journals, and attend occasional conferences of workers in your field.

2. Take courses to brush up on old skills or learn new ones. Such courses are offered by many community colleges as well as by the extension departments of colleges and universities.

3. Attend lectures or workshops related to your occupation. Besides helping to refresh your memory about work subjects, attending such meetings may put you in touch with people in your field who may be able to supply future job leads.

4. Practice your skills through volunteer or club activities. Many community organizations need persons who can raise funds, organize activities, write reports or brochures, type, answer correspondence, publicize upcoming events, keep financial records, or do other administrative tasks. In addition, volunteers are needed in many areas or fields directly related to work specialties. Recreation workers can use their skills in Scout work, for example, and teachers can tutor or volunteer for other educational programs.

By helping you maintain old skills or learn new ones that will be your passport to future employment, the preceding activities can also help give you the confidence you will need to look for a job after an absence from the work world. Lack of self-confidence and lack of skills are major stumbling blocks to women who do not plan job reentry in advance.

Should You Be a Working Mother?

A final word about decisions concerning work and motherhood is in order here, and that word is "guilt." Strong schools of thought exist on the subject of working mothers. Some people firmly believe that working mothers cheat themselves of the joys of watching children grow and deprive their children of adequate care. Others are equally convinced that mothers who do not work rob themselves of a life outside the family, cheat society by not using skills valued in the workplace, or tend to smother their children with more attention and concern than is healthy for a youngster. A case can be made for either viewpoint, and many women who choose one course of action are susceptible to guilt feelings when they hear the opposing point of view. They may question their own decisions and wonder if they might be better mothers if they adopted another course.

But there is no right answer to the question of whether mothers should or should not work. Mothers are individuals, each with her own unique needs. You have no reason to feel guilty about making whatever decisions concerning work and motherhood are most satisfying for you within your family situation. This decision, like all career decisions, is apt to fit best if you custom-tailor it to suit yourself. You are the person who must live your life, and you are the person your decisions should please.

Happy career planning and the best of luck!

References

Roesch, Roberta, *Women in Action,* John Day Company, New York City, 1967.

U.S. Department of Labor, Bureau of Labor Statistics, *Occupational Outlook Handbook, 1974–75 Edition,* 1974.

U.S. Department of Labor, Women's Bureau, *Job Horizons for College Women,* 1967.